Your Missouri Courts

Case.net

Search for Cases by: Select Search Method...

09MR-CV00391-02 - MO. F.S.D. V JEFFREY W MCBRIDE &

Case Header	Parties & Attorneys	Docket Entries	Charges, Judgments & Sentences	Service Information	Filings Due	Scheduled Hearings & Trials	Civil Judgments	Garnishments/ Execution

Sort Date Entries: ● Descending ○ Ascending   Display Options: All Entries

04/30/2015	**Correspondence Sent**
	copy of Judgment mailed to both parties at last known addresses copy mailed to FSPC copy given to Atty Rapp
	Judgment Entered
	#26 Judgment Terminating Child Support on Ava entered as per memo JUDGE JOHN J JACKSON
04/29/2015	**Affidavit of Termination CS**
	#25 Acknowledgment Agreeing to Termination of Child Support on ●●● 08/21/07 ●●●●●●●●●/CP filed AFFIDAVIT DATE
	Filed By: ●●●●● IRENE ●●●● STARTS AT DOB OF CHILD
04/16/2015	**Return Service on Affidavit**
	#24 Affidavit for Termination of Child Support returned by Marion County Sheriff showing service to Respondent on 4/15/15 filed. Document ID - 15-SAFI-1, Served To - ●●●●● ●●●●● IRENE. Server - SO MARION COUNTY-PALMYRA, Served Date - 15-APR-15; Served Time - 15:08:00; Service Type - Sheriff Department, Reason Description - Served
04/14/2015	**Affidavit Issued**
	Document ID - 15-SAFI-1, for ●●●●● ●●●●●●●● ←
03/25/2015	**Affidavit of Termination CS**
	#23 ←
	Filed By: JEFFREY W MCBRIDE

EVERYONE HAS THE RIGHT TO DUE PROCESS AND TO FACE THEIR ACCUSSERS.

CHILD SUPPORT IS A CASE THAT IS BEING HEARD WITHOUT YOU THERE. THIS IS FRAUD AND VIOLATES YOUR RIGHTS.

The U.S. national debt exceeded $28 trillion in 2021. One thing that many people may not know is that the Social Security Trust Fund owns

a significant portion of that national debt.

So how does that work and what does it mean? Below we'll dive into who actually owns the U.S. national debt and how that impacts you.

2 Categories of the National Debt

The U.S. Treasury manages the U.S. debt through its Bureau of the Public Debt. The debt falls into two categories: intragovernmentalholdings and debt held by the public.

Public Debt

The public holds over $22 trillion of the national debt.[1] Foreign governments hold a large portion of the public debt, while the rest is owned by U.S. banks and investors, the Federal Reserve, state and localgovernments, mutual funds, pensions funds, insurance companies, andsavings bonds.

The Treasury breaks down who holds how much of the public debt in aquarterly Treasury Bulletin. In its September 2021 bulletin, which included data through March 2021, foreign and international investors held over $7 trillion, while state and local governments held $1.17 trillion and mutual funds were $3.6 trillion. Other holders of the publicdebt include insurance companies, U.S. savings bonds, private pensionfunds, and other holders, including individuals, government-sponsoredenterprises, brokers and dealers, banks, bank personal trusts and estates, corporate and non-corporate businesses, and other investors.

BUT ONE MOST OVERSTAND OF WHAT THIS HAPPENS FIRST.

ALL COURTS ARE BANKS AND HAVE CLERKS BENCH MEANS BANC. ALL COURTS ARE TAX COURTS ACCORDING TO 28 U.S.C. 3002 (2) UNLESS IT IS CREATED BY CONGRESS AND CONGRESS HAS A VALID CASE FOR YOU.THE US DEPARTMENT OF TREASURY IS THE BOOKKEEPERS FOR THE UNITED STATES CORPORATION

UNLESS YOU RECORD THE RETURN OR THE TAX THEN THEY CAN NOT DO THE BOOKKEEPING ON IT.

THAT'S WHY THE TREASURYS BOOKS ARE OFF BALANCED THE PAYABLES AND RECEIVEABLES ARE OFF BALANCED UP BECAUSE THEY CAN NOT PAY THE PAYABLES WHICH IS DUE TO THE PEOPLE.

THEY CAN NOT PAY THE PEOPLE BECAUSE THEY HAVE NOT FILED THE CORRECT PAPERWORK TO GET THE REFUND ON THE CREDIT THAT THEY ARE GIVING AWAY

AFTER 36 MONTHS THE CORPORATIONS AND BANKERS COME IN AS THE NOMINEE AND USE YOUR TAX PAYER IDENTIFCATION NUMBER ON A 1099A UTLIZING THE DEBT INSTRUMENT AS ABANDONED PROPERTY BECAUSE YOU NEVER CLAIMED IT. WHO EVER CLAIMS IT OWNS IT

WE ALSO SEND THEM A BLANK W9 REQUESTING TO SEE THEIR TAX IDENTIFICATION NUMBER AS YOU FILL THIS OUT WHEN STARTING ANY NEW BANK ACCOUNT. WE ATTACH THIS TO ANY FORMS WHEN DEALING WITH CORPORATIONS UTLIZING OUR CREDIT.

THE AMOUNTS BELONGING TO ANOTHER PERSON IS THE AMOUNT OF THE CREDIT THEY ARE USING AND THAT SHALL BE REPRESENTED AS A TAX WHEN THE TAX IS ASSESSED IT THEN BECOMES A TAX ISSUE AND TAX MATTER AND THEN IT BECOMES A RETURN. WHEN YOU SHOW THE CORPORATIONS AS RECEIPENTS OF THE

FUNDS THEN THE IRS SHALL ISSUE YOU A REFUND. IF YOU DO NOT DO THIS THEN YOU ABANDON THE FUNDS AND THE 1099 A IS FILED BY THE CORPORATIONS AND THE FUNDS GOTO THE CORPORATION THAT FILED THE 1099 A. THE CORPORATIONS ARE ALWAYS FILING AS A NOMINEE FOR THE TRUE OWNER WHEN YOU SIGN OVER THE RIGHTS TO YOUR BUSINESS (YOUR NAME AND CREDIT).

EVERYTHING IS A TAX ISSUE UNDER THE BANKRUPTCY OF THE UNITED STATES CORPORATIONS.

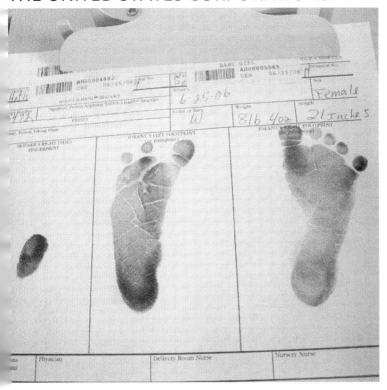

The sole proprietorship is the simplest
business form under which one can operate a
business. The sole proprietorship is not a
legal entity. It simply refers to a person who
owns the business and is personally
responsible for its debts. A sole
proprietorship can operate under the name
of its owner or it can do business under a
fictitious name, such as Nancy's Nail Salon.
The fictitious name is simply a trade name--
it does not create a legal entity separate from the sole proprietor owner.

The sole proprietorship is a popular business form due to its simplicity, ease of setup,
and nominal cost. A sole proprietor need only register his or her name and secure local
licenses, and the sole proprietor is ready for business. A distinct disadvantage,
however, is that the owner of a sole proprietorship remains personally liable for all the
business's debts. So, if a sole proprietor business runs into financial trouble, creditors
can bring lawsuits against the business owner. If such suits are successful, the owner
will have to pay the business debts with his or her own money.

WHEN YOU ARE BORN A BIRTH CERTIFICATE IS CREATED.
A BIRTH CERTIFICATE IS JUST SIMPLY PUT A TITLE OF
OWNERSHIP WHICH HAS CREATED BENEFICIAL INTEREST
WITHIN EVERYTHING YOU SHALL OWN. SOLE MEANS
ONE HENCE SOLE PROP THEY PROP THE SOLE OF YOUR
FOOT AND AS SOON AS THE SOCIAL SECURITY NUMBER
IS ESTABLISHED YOUR TAXPAYER IDENTIFCATION
NUMBER THIS IS YOUR PRIVATE BANKING NUMBER SET
UP FOR THE SOCIALIST SECURITY ADMINISTRATION
WHICH IS ANOTHER TRUST. THE BENEFITS ARE TIED TO
YOU BEING ABLE TO UTILZE TRUST CERTIFICATE UNITS

FROM THE FEDERAL RESERVES WHICH IS UNDER THE IN GOD WE TRUST YES THAT IS THE NAME OF THEIR TRUST THE IN GOD WE.

THE CONSTITUTION IS CONSIDERED TO BE AN EXPRESSED TRUST. WHEN YOU GO INTO ANY COURT ROOM YOU ARE CREATING A CONSTRUCTIVE TRUST. THIS IS A DIFFERENT TOPIC FOR A DIFFERENT BOOK BUT AS OF RIGHT NOW LETS STICK TO THE SOLE PROP BUSINESS AND THE TAX.

28 U.S. Code § 3002. Definitions

(2) "Court" means any court created by the Congress of the United States, excluding the United States Tax Court.

(3) "Debt" means—

  (A) an amount that is owing to the United States on account of a direct loan, or loan insured or guaranteed, by the United States; or

AS YOU CAN SEE ALL COURTS ARE TAX COURTS AND ALL DEBTS ARE OWED TO THE UNITED STATES CORPORATION. IF YOU CONTINUE TO READ TO SECTION 15 YOU SHALL SEE THAT THE UNITED STATES IS INDEED A CORPORATION.

(4) "Debtor" means a person who is liable for a debt or against w claim for a debt.

(5) "Disposable earnings" means that part of earnings remaining deductions required by law have been withheld.

(6) "Earnings" means compensation paid or payable for personal denominated as wages, salary, commission, bonus, or otherwise, periodic payments pursuant to a pension or retirement program.

(7) "Garnishee" means a person (other than the debtor) who has thought to have, possession, custody, or control of any property ii debtor has a substantial nonexempt interest, including any obligat debtor or to become due the debtor, and against whom a garnishr section 3104 or 3205 is issued by a court.

(9) "Nonexempt disposable earnings" means 25 percent of disposable earnings, subject to section 303 of the Consumer Credit Protection Act.

(10) "Person" includes a natural person (including an individual Indian), a corporation, a partnership, an unincorporated association, a trust, or an estate, or any other public or private entity, including a State or local government or an Indian tribe.

(11) "Prejudgment remedy" means the remedy of attachment, receivership, garnishment, or sequestration authorized by this chapter to be granted before judgment on the merits of a claim for a debt.

(12) "Property" includes any present or future interest, whether legal or equitable, in real, personal (including choses in action), or mixed property, tangible or intangible, vested or contingent, wherever located and however held (including community property and property held in trust (including spendthrift and pension trusts)), but excludes—

(13) "Security agreement" means an agreement that creates or provides for a lien.

(14) "State" means any of the several States, the District of Columbia, the Commonwealth of Puerto Rico, the Commonwealth of the Northern Marianas, or any territory or possession of the United States.

(15) "United States" means—

    (A) a Federal corporation;

    (B) an agency, department, commission, board, or other entity of the United States; or

    (C) an instrumentality of the United States.

(16) "United States marshal" means a United States marshal, a deputy marshal, or an official of the United States Marshals Service designated under section 564.

ALSO A NOTE TO MENTION SECTION 10 PERSON MEANS CORPORATION. THEN AGAIN THIS WHY YOU ARE CONSIDERED

A SOLE PROP CORPORATION AND YOUR BODY, LABOR AND EVEN WELL BEING CAN BE ATTACHED AS COLLATERAL FOR ANYMISHAPS OF THE BUSINESS DUE TO YOU NOT HAVING PROPERSTANDING BY UPDATING YOUR STATUS WHICH WE HIGHLY RECOMMEND YOU DO BEFORE MOVING FORWARD WITH ANY 1099 OID PROCESS. WE ALSO HAVE ANOTHER BOOK ON HOW TO UPDATE YOUR STATUS PROPERLY ON THE PUBLIC SIDE ANDTHE PRIVATE SIDE.

AS YOUR BIRTH CERTIFICATE IS THE TITLE THAT SHOWS BENEFICIAL OWNERSHIP SO THIS IS THE PRIVATE SIDE. THE PUBLIC SIDE IS THE MONEY HOW ARE YOU ACTING IN WHAT CHARACTER OR TITLE ARE YOU ACTING FROM. WITH A SOCIAL YOU ARE A SLAVE. AS SOCIAL WORK FOR THE EIN THE EMPLOYER IDENTIFICATION NUMBER. EMPLOYEES ARE SLAVESAND THE EMPLOYERS ARE THE MASTERS. AS THE SOCIAL NUMBER AS WORKS FOR THE EIN.

FROM A LIMITED LIABILTY COMPANY YOU WOULD ACT FROM A MEMBER OR JUST AN AUTHORIZED REPRESENTIVE SO TO SPEAK. WITH CORPORATIONS YOU ACT FORM A CHIEF EXECUTIVE STANDPOINT OR EVEN PRESIDENT OR VICE PRESIDENT. FROM THE TRUST STANDPOINT YOU ALWAYS OPERATE FROM THE GRANTOR OR ADMINSTRATOR WHEN DEALING WITH YOUR PRIVATE AFFAIRS WITHIN A PUBLIC PLAY.

Why is this important when dealing with child support?

Because A PARENT is a PAIR WHO RENTS.

CHILDREN means PROPERTY OF A COPORATION.

So you are a corporation and so is your children that belong to the United States INC.

Only a live man can state a claim to this property so it is important to not be the business but in control of the business.

First establish an E.I.N. and this is free. I myself like to do Irrevocable trust or just a regular E.I.N. as my names as the business. Get a virtual address I like ipostal1.com and viola you have a business.

But there is a few more steps to make it official and have a status change to have standing in your state and local jurisdiction.

Go to your secretary of state website an open up the LLC company within your state. Fees will be attached with this but this will give you standing in law within the state.

Secondly open up a business name in your children's name owned by your new LLC company that you made your name.

That's right your name as a business will own your children's name.

Remember you believe they have power due to publications if you own the name then they are violating copyright laws because you now own the name.

What I do is make my children's name a Doing Business As Name or a Fictitious name in other states It is called and make it owned by name that is now the llc.

FATHERS NAME LLC OWNS THE CHILDRENS NAME (DBA)

ANOTHER WAY IS OPEN A SERIES LLC AND MAKE THE KIDS NAME UNDER A DIFFERENT SERIES AND THIS WOULD BE DONE UNDER YOU OPERATING AGREEMENTS.

I feel the first way is quicker and more efficient.

There is always an admin process at first.

However Have Fun and relax.

Child support is a tanf grant and a grant does not have to ever be paid back. Tanf is what truly pays for child support and is also apart of the food stamp program in most states.

Please soak this knowledge in read it over and over until it makes sense. Me personally once I send my paperwork in I no Longer goto court.

If they send me any papework in the mail that isn't certified mail I send it back and Mark on it refuse to contract return to sender all rights reserved and black out my name since they are in violation of copyright laws by publishing my business name without my permission.

COURT CLERK MUST FILE YOUR DOCUMENTS

The minute you receive any affidavit, it is recorded. Should you refuse to record my affidavits, or any other documents, once deposited with you, you are committing a crime against justice under Statutes at Large Sec. 5403 and it is punishable by up to a two thousand dollar ($2,000.00) fine and three (3) years imprisonment. If your county attorney told you not to file any documents like mine, you are still responsible, as I do not accept any third party interveners. Any attorney, district attorney, or anyone form the lawyering craft are all third parties and do not have a license to make a legal determination in this matter as they do not represent Me and you, the county clerk, and do not have the authority to represent Me.

Federal Rules of Civil Procedure 5(d)(4) Acceptance by the clerk. A clerk must not refuse to file a paper solely because it is not in the form prescribed by these rules or by local rule or practice.

A court clerk does not have the authority to make any judicial decisions about your paperwork or case. His/Her duties are ministerial and not tribunal. The tribunal is who gets to make the decisions regarding the quality of a paper. The clerk must file your papers on demand. Send by Registered Mail if he/she continues to refuse to comply.

Anyone who removes a document from the record can be punished for up to three (3) years in prison according to 18 USC 2071.

18 USC 2071 – (a) Whoever wilfully and unlawfully conceals, removes, mutilates, obliterates, or destroys, or attempts to do so, or, with intent to do so takes and carries away any record, proceeding, map, book, paper, document, or other thing, filed or deposited with any clerk or officer of any court of the United States, or in any public office, or with any judicial or public officer of the United States, shall be fined under this title or imprisoned not more than three (3) years, or both.

(b) Whoever, having the custody of any such record, proceeding, map, book, document, paper, or other thing, wilfully and unlawfully conceals, removes, mutilates, obliterates, falsifies, or destroys the same, shall be fined under this title or imprisoned not more than three (3) years, or both; and shall forfeit his office and be disqualified from holding any office under the United States. As used in this subsection, the term "office" does not include the office held by any person as a retired officer of the Armed Forces of the United States.

A document is filed once it is delivered to the clerk. It does not have to be stamped and signed. The court has held that a document is filed even if delivered to a deputy clerk at night at his home.

"…it is settled law that delivery of a pleading to a proper official is sufficient to constitute filing thereof. United States v. Lombardo, 241 U.S. 73, 36 S. Ct. 508, 60 L.Ed. 897 (1916); Milton v. United States, 105 F.2d 253, 255 (5th Cir 1939). In Greeson v.

Sherman, 265 F. Supp. 340 (D.C.Va. 1967) it was held that a pleading delivered to a deputy clerk at his home at night was thereby "filed." (Freeman v. Giacomo Costa Fu Adrea, 282 F. Supp. 525 (E.D.Pa. 04/5/1968).

The clerk of a court, like the Recorder is required to accept documents filed. It is no incumbent upon him to judicially determine the legal significance of the tendered documents. In re Halladjian, 174 F. 834 (C.C.Mass.1909); United States, to Use of Kinney v. Bell, 127 F. 1002 (C.C.E.D.Pa.1904); State ex rel. Kaufman v. Sutton, 231 So.2d 874 (Fla.App.1970); Malinou v. McElroy, 99 R.I. 277, 207 A.2d 44 (1965); State ex rel. Wanamaker v. Miller, 164 Ohio St. 176, 177, 128 N.E.2d 110 (1955).) (Daniel K. Mayers Et Al., v. Peter S. Ridley Et Al. No. 71-1418 (06/30/72, United States Court of Appeals for the DC Circuit.) (Emphasis added)

"An instrument is deemed in law filed at the time it is delivered to the clerk, regardless of whether the instrument is filemarked." Biffle v. Morton Rubber Indus. Inc., 785 S.W.2d 143, 144 (Tex. 1990)

The minute all documents are received, it is recorded. Refusal to record documents once deposited to the county recorder s considered criminal subject to Title 18 USC 2071 and it is punishable by fines and imprisonment without regard to third party intervention and where consent to their party intervention is refused by the party recording the document.

Revised Statutes of The United States, 1st session, 43 Congress 1873-1874.
Title LXX.---CRIMES.---CH. 4 CRIMES AGAINST JUSTICE
SEC. 5403. (Destroying, &c., public records.)
Every person who wilfully destroys or attempts to destroy, or, with intent to steal or destroy, takes and carries away any record, paper, or proceeding of a court of justice, filed or deposited with any clerk or officer of such court, or any paper, or document, or record filed or deposited in any public office, or with any judicial or public officer, shall, without reference to the value of the record, paper, document, or proceeding so taken, pay a fine of not more than two thousand dollars, or suffer imprisonment, at hard labor, not more than three years, or both: (See §§ 5408, 5411, 5412.1)

SEC. 5407. (Conspiracy to defeat enforcement of the laws.)
If two or more persons in any State or Territory conspire for the purpose of impeding, hindering, obstructing, or defeating, in any manner, the due course of justice in any State or Territory, with intent to deny to any citizen the equal protection of the laws, or to injure him or his property for lawfully enforcing, or attempting to enforce, the right of any person, or class of persons, to the equal protection of the laws, each of such persons shall be punished by a fine of not less than five hundred nor more than five thousand dollars, or by imprisonment, with or without hard labor, not less than six months or by both such fine and imprisonment. See §§ 1977-1991, 2004-2010, 5506-5510.1

SEC. 5408. (Destroying record by officer in charge.)
Every officer, having the custody of any record, document, paper, or proceeding specified in section fifty-four hundred and three, who fraudulently takes away, or withdraws, or

destroys any such record, document, paper, or proceeding filed in his office or deposited with him or in his custody, shall pay a fine of not more than two thousand dollars, or suffer imprisonment at hard labor not more than three years, or both-, and shall, moreover, forfeit his office and be forever afterward disqualified from holding any office under the Government of the United States.

The Oath of Office is a quid pro quo contract (U.S. Const. Art. 6, Clauses 2 and 3, Davis v. Lawyers Surety Corporation, 459 SW2d 655, 657., Tex. Civ. App. In which clerks, officials, or officers of the government pledge to perform (Support and uphold the United States and State Constitutions) in return for substance (wages, perks, benefits). Proponents are subjected to the penalties and remedies for Breach of Contract, conspiracy under Titled 28 U.S.C. Sections 241, 242., treason under the Constitution at Article 3, Section 3., and intrinsic fraud as per Auerbach vs. Samuels., 10 Utah 2nd 152, 349 P. 2nd 1112, 1114, Alleghany Corp vs. Kirby, D.C.N.Y. 218 F. Supp. 164, 183, and Keeton Packing Co. vs. State, 437 S.W. 20, 28.

Violation	Code Section	Recommended Penalty
Breach of Oath Contract	18 USC 3571	$250,000.00 (each violation)
Denial of proper Warrant	18 USC 3571	$250,000.00 (each violation)

(no supporting affidavit, no Miranda Warning / no damaged complaining party & etc.)

Denial of Claim of Special Appearance	18 USC 3571	$250,000.00 (each violation)
Denial of Reasonable Defense Arguments	18 USC 3571	$250,000.00 (each violation)
Denial of Access to All Evidence	18 USC 3571	$250,000.00 (each violation)
Attempted Slavery	18 USC 3571	$250,000.00 (each violation)

(Forced Compliance to [adhesion] Contracts not held) Example: Requiring a citizen to participate in the Federal Reserve Banking System/Conversion of the Constitutional Right to Travel to a State Privilege i.e. no auto tag, no compulsory insurance, no inspection sticker failure to fasten a seatbelt, failure to stop for inspection, search without proper warrant, etc.
Converting a Constitutional Right to a

State granted Privilege with above	18 USC 3571	$250,000.00 (each violation)
Denial of Provision in the Constitution	18 USC 3571	$250,000.00 (each violation)

(US and/or State. Example: Demanding worthless unbacked printed paper (must be coined) FRN's payment of state debts. Clerk proceeding with a foreclosure where the filing fee was not paid in lawful money of substance gold or silver specie coinage in violation of Article 1, Section 10, Clause 1 (a federal injunction))

Treason (combined above acts)	18 USC 3571	$250,000.00 (each violation)

Falsifying jurisdiction (trying a common law matter under colourable maritime) trying a state matter under false color of jurisdiction in the U.S. District Court outside of the 10-square mile provision at Article 1, Section 8, Clause 17)

Attempted Genocide	18 USC 1091	$1,050,000.00 (each violation)

(destroying a family, their way to earn a living while taking their home under color of law and pretended law)

Misprison of Felony	18 USC 4	$500.00 (each violation)
Conspiracy (2 or more people)	18 USC 241	$10,000.00 (each violation)

Attempted Extortion	18 USC 872	$5,000.00 (each violation)

(Claiming a debt not owed under the U.S. or State Constitutions) Example: collecting a form of taxes, i.e. Property/Automobile taxes not authorize by the U.S. Constitution. (Holding a Certified Money Order and pretending it does not exist, a felony as per U.S. v. Tweel, 550 F.2d 297, 299, 300.

Mail Fraud and Mail Threats	18 USC 876	$5,000.00 (each violation)
Fraud	18 USC 1001	$5,000.00 (each violation)
Falsification of Documents	18 USC 1001	$5,000.00 (each violation)
Perjury	18 USC 1621	$5,000.00 (each violation)
Subordinating of Perjury	18 USC 1621	$5,000.00 (each violation)
Grand Theft		
(see no. of counts 18 USC 2112)	18 USC 3571	$5,000.00 (each violation)
Racketeering (Civil)	18 USC 1694	$25,000.00 (each violation)
Racketeering (Criminal)	18 USC 1963	$250,000.00 (each violation)
Concealment, removal, mutilation	18 USC 2071	(look up for $ amount)

Failure to produce said documents guarantees the process of due process of law and your removal from office, in addition to, statutory penalty, punishment and possible incarceration. This evidence has also been forwarded to the Internal Revenue Service Criminal Investigation Division, along with a copy of the stolen document, as the taxation for the fine in the amount of $_____constitutes perusal by the provost marshall(s) as such.

The fines incumbent to the documents filed are in the amount of $_____. Having engaged in the commerce to infringe upon this lawful declaration, forms 1099OID will be filed with the Internal Revenue Service to have this fine enforced and to have the Internal Revenue Service require you to pay this by tax.

A clerk of court is an officer of the court who has charge of its clerical business and keeps its records and seal, issues process, enters judgments and orders, makes certified copies from the record, etc. He belongs to the judicial department of the government. People ex rel. Vanderburg v. Brady, 275 Ill 261, 114 NE 25.

A clerk of court is a person employed in a public office of the court whose duty it is to keep the records or accounts of the court. Jones v. Reed, 58 Ga.App. 72, 197 SE 665.

The duties of clerks of court are in general to serve the court in a ministerial capacity, to act as custodian of its records, and to perform such duties as are prescribed by law or imposed by the lawful authority of the court. Union Bank & Trust Co. v. County of Los Angeles, 2 Cal.App.2d 600, 38 P.2d 442 (ovrld on the grounds Minsky v. Los Angeles, 11 Cal.3d 113, 113 Cal.Rptr. 102, 520 P.2d 726.

In the performance of his duties as a ministerial officer of the court, the clerk is subject to the control of the court. See State ex rel. Caldwell v. Cockrell, 280 Mo 269, 217 SW 524;

State ex rel. Tolls v. Tolls, 160 Or 317, 85 P.2d 366, 119 ALR 1370 (ovrld on the grounds Burnett v. Hatch, 200 Or 291, 266 P.2d 414).

If the clerk fails to obey an order of the court, he may be guilty of contempt (see Shelley v. Thomas, 232 Ala 227, 167 So 316; Ex parte Thatcher, 7 Ill. 167; State ex rel. Caldwell v. Cockrell, 280 Mo 269, 217 SW 524; Territory v. Clancy 7 NM 580, 37 P 1108) even when the order is erroneous in law (The fact that a court order requiring payment of accrued temporary alimony and suit money is not properly a judgment constituting a lien on realty and on which execution may be issued does not prevent the clerk's refusal to obey the court's direction to docket it in the judgment lien docket from being a contempt. State ex rel. Tolls v. Tolls, 160 Or 317, 85 P.2d 366, 119 ALR 1370 (ovrld on the grounds Burnett v. Hatch, 200 Or. 291, 266 P.2d 414).

A clerk of court may not exercise judicial power except by constitutional or legislative provision (see Gardner v. Bunn, 132 Ill 403, 23 NE 1072; Re Terrill, 52 Kan 29, 34 P 457; Hornack v. State, 39 Ohio App 203, 177 NE 244. It is well settled tat although a clerk of court may perform acts of ministerial and nondiscretionary character with respect to judicial proceedings, such clerk has no judicial powers in the absence of specific statutory or constitutional authority. State ex rel. Citizens Nat. Bank v. Superior Court of Madison County, 236 Ind. 135, 138 N.E.2d 900) and then only in accordance with the strict language of the provision (see Pacific Nat. Fire Ins. Co. v. Irmiger, 254 Wis 207, 36 N.W.2d 89. When judicial or quasi-judicial powers are expressly conferred upon the clerk of court, the clerk's authority is strictly limited within the terms of the statutory or constitutional provision conferring it. State ex rel. Citizens Nat. Bank v. Superior Court of Madison County, 236 Ind. 135, 138 N.E.2d 900).

A clerk of court cannot ordinarily perform functions of a purely judicial character, such as the determination of the sufficiency of a complaint (see Newport v. Culbreath, 120 Fla 152, 162 So. 340).

It is the official duty of the clerk of court to file all papers in a cause presented by the parties, and to indorse the correct date of the filing thereon. (See Brinson v. Georgia R. Bank & Trust Co., 45 Ga.App. 459, 165, SE 321. Under the statute, the clerk's duties include the obligation to file all papers properly before him. See Hamilton v. Department of Industry, Labor & Human Relations, 56 Wes.2d 673, 203 NW2d 7 (ovrld on other grounds Re Pewaukee (Wis) 241 NW2d 603).

As a ministerial officer, it is the mandatory duty of the clerk of the Court of Civil Appeals to file and forward to the Supreme Court any document tendered to him appertaining to an appeal in any cause pending in that court which is addressed to the Supreme Court. (See Wagner v. Garrett, 114 Tex. 362, 269 SW 1030).

A paper is filed with the clerk of court when it is delivered to him for that purpose. (See Morthland v.Lincoln Nat. Life Ins. Co., 220 Ind 692, 42 NE2d 41, reh den 220 Ind 734, 46 NE2d 203).

It is the duty of the clerk of court, in the absence of instructions from the court to the contrary, to accept for filing any paper presented to him provided such paper is not scurrilous or obscene, is properly prepared, and is accompanied by the requisite filing fee. (See State ex rel. Wanamaker v. Miller, 164 Ohio St 174, 57 Ohio Ops 151, 128 NE2d 108.

When the statute requires the clerk of court to file all papers delivered to him to be filed, he is not concerned with the merit of the papers nor with their effect and interpretation. (See Corey v. Carback, 201 Md 389, 94 A2d 629).

It is not incumbent upon one who has the ministerial function of accepting the filing of a complaint to judicially determine the legal significance of the tendered document. See State ex rel. Kaufman v. Sutton (Fla.App.)231 So2d 874.

The clerk has <u>no discretion</u> in the matter of filing papers recognized by law as properly belonging in the record of causes. (See Bernard v. Crowell (Tex Civ App), 38 SW2d 912).

It is <u>not</u> for the clerk to inquire into the purpose or contents of such papers, or into the circumstances giving rise to them or attending their preparation. (See Bernard v. Crowell (Tex Civ App), 38 SW2d 912 (bystander's bill of exceptions).

The power to make any decision as to the propriety of any paper submitted, or as to the right of a person to file such paper, is <u>vested in the court, not the clerk</u>. (See State ex rel. Wanamaker v. Miller, 164 Ohio St 176, 57 Ohio Ops 151, 128 NE2d 108).

Those dealing with the clerk of a court concerning an action or matter then ending have a right to expect that he will perform the ministerial duties connected with his office, and his neglect or failure to do so should not prejudice their rights. (See Williams v. Tyler, 14 Ala App. 591, 71 So 51, cert den 198 Ala 696, 73 So 1002; Hogs Back Consol. Mining Co. v. New Basil Consol. Gravel Mining Co. 65 Cal 22, 2 P 489; Silverman v. Childs, 107 Ill. App. 52; May v. Wolvington, 69 Md 117, 14 A 706; Thompson v. Sharp, 17 Neb 69, 22 NW 78; Hopkins v. Giggli (Tex) 6 SW 625; Black v. Hurlbut, 73 Wis 126, 40 NW 673).

A clerk of court is, generally speaking, liable personally and on his official bond to a litigant injured as a result of his negligence or misconduct.

The principle that a public officer should be held to a faithful performance of his official duties and made to answer in damages to all persons who may have been injured through his malfeasance, omission, or neglect applies to the negligence, carelessness, or misconduct of a clerk of court. (See 63 Am Jr 2d, Public Officers and Employees §§ 287 et seq. Also see Lick v. Madden, 36 Cal. 208).

As a public ministerial officer, the clerk is answerable for any act of negligence or misconduct in office resulting in injury to the complaining party. (See Eslava v. Jones, 83

Ala 139, 3 So 317; Stewart v. Sholl, 99 Ga 534, 26 SE 757; Stine v. Shuttle, 134 Ind. App. 67, 186 NE2d 168; Selover v. Sheardown, 73 Minn 393, 76 NW 50; State ex rel. St. Louis v. Priest, 348 Mo 37, 152 SW2d 109.

Clerks of the Superior Court are no less liable for the negligent performance of their official duties than for a failure to perform such duties. Touchton v. Echols County, 211 Ga 85, 84 SE2d 81.

A clerk of court is liable in a civil action for a negligent omission to perform a statutory duty which proximately causes injury to another, unless the injured party was contributorily negligent. Maddox v. Astro Invest., 45 Ohio App 2d 203, 74 Ohio Ops 2d 312, 343 NE2d 133.

DIRECTIONS FOR CASES

GET ALL DOCUMENTS NOTARAZIED

AFTER NOTARIZED

PUT TWO CENT STAMPS OR ANY STAMP WITH A NUMERIC VALUE NOT A FOREVER STAMP AND PLACE IT ON TOP RIGHT OF DOCUMENTS

AUTOGRAPH THRU THE STAMPS

AUTOGRAPH THE BACK OF THE DOCUMENT LIKE A CHECK

AUTOGRAPH AND DATE ALL RIGHTS RESERVED WITHOUT PREJUDICE

Attach form 56 fill out like illustration

Attach w9 and 1099 oid and grant form 990 THEY ARE TO BE LEFT BLANK

 YOU CAN FILL IN THE sf 28 forms OR LEAVE blank

Attach promissory note as well and AUTOGRAPH and date back like a check

You no longer have to goto court return all mail to sender after blacking out YOUR NAME AS IT IS YOUR

NAME AND CAN NOT BE USED WITHOUT YOUR PERMISSION

SEND CERTIFIED MAIL TO THE CLERK OF CLERKS

MAKE SURE TO SENT TO HER NAME

EXAMPLE

Jane Doe d/b/a Illinois County Clerk

Then I would send a copy to the Federal District Courts Since they buy up the bonds and child support is a federal grant.

The State's Attorney as only Attorneys can give back rights during a war which this is a war as they are versus your estate.

Then I would start my 1099 OID process found in another book and send the case to the IRS the real court which is a tax court!

Then I would send copies to the Security Exchange Commission, The Federal and Trade Commission

And then The General Service Administration,

This is not legal advice if you need legal advice please seek counsel this is for educational and informational and entertainment purposes only

AFFIDAVIT OF FACTS

A MAN :JOHN DOE - JR OF THE FAMILY: BADY,

PURSUANT IDAHO STATE STATUTES AND UNITED STATES CONSTITUTIONS AS WELL

AS 45 C.F.R. § 303.101(c)(4) REQUIRES THIS COURT *OBSTA PRINCIPIIS* AND JUDICIAL

REVIEW OF FACTS AND EVIDENCE OR LACK OF EVIDENCE DE:JOHN DOE - JR OF THE

FAMILY: BADY, DING IMMEDIATE DISMISSAL AND DISCHARGE OF ALL SUPPORT

ORDERS CREATED BY EXPEDITED PROCESSES IN THIS COURT. THE SUPPORT

ORDERS WERE CREATED WITHOUT DUE PROCESS OF LAW, A FUNDAMENTAL

REQUIREMENT BEFORE LIFE, LIBERTY, AND PROPERTY CAN BE DEPRIVED. SUPPORT

ORDERS USED TO DEPRIVE

A :JOHN DOE - JR OF THE FAMILY: BADY, ; :JOHN DOE - Jr of The Family:

Bady, PROPERTY IS A CLEAR VIOLATION OF DUE PROCESS OF LAW UNDER 5TH

AND 14TH AMENDMENTS AND EXPEDITED PROCESSES UNDER 45 CFR § 303.101(c)(4).

THIS DE:JOHN DOE - JR OF THE FAMILY: BADY, D FOR DISMISSAL AND DISCHARGE IS

WITHOUT TIME RESTRAINTS FOR THE SUPPORT ORDERS BEING USED TO DEPRIVE

THE PROPERTY OF A :JOHN DOE - JR OF THE FAMILY: BADY, ; :JOHN DOE - Jr

of The Family: Bady, WERE CREATED IN VIOLATION OF DUE PROCESS OF LAW,

AND ANY JUDGMENT MADE IN VIOLATION OF DUE PROCESS OF LAW IS A VOID
JUDGMENT. VOID JUDGMENTS, PURSUANT

THE SUPREME COURT OF THE UNITED STATES ARE NULLITIES WHICH CAN BE

ATTACKED DIRECTLY OR COLLATERALLY AT ANY TIME IN ANY COURT. THIS

DE:JOHN DOE - JR OF THE FAMILY: BADY, D FOR DISMISSAL AND DISCHARGE

IS REQUIRING THIS COURT TO REMEDY BY IMMEDIATELY DISMISSING AND

DISCHARGING SUPPORT ORDERS WITH PREJUDICE.

PURSUANT 45 CFR § 303.101(c)(4) THE SUPPORT HEARINGS ARE EXPEDITED PROCESSES

REQUIRING DUE PROCESS AND EQUAL PROTECTION OF LAW FOLLOWED BY

JUDICIAL REVIEW AND CONFIRMATION BEFORE ANY SUPPORT ORDERS MAY BE

RENDERED TO START THE PROCESS OF DEPRIVING PROPERTY FOR CHILD SUPPORT.

THE JUDICIAL CONFIRMATION OF SUPPORT ORDERS WERE NOT FOLLOWED

RENDERING ALL SUPPORT ORDERS VOID WITHOUT LEGAL FORCE.

CHILD SUPPORT MUST BE PROVEN BY PATERNITY TESTING
OR PATERNITY ACKNOWLEDGEMENT. WITHOUT CONFIRMED PATERNITY

ANY SUPPORT ORDER IS VOID WITHOUT LEGAL FORCE.

THE SUPPORT ORDERS USED TO DEPRIVE PROPERTY OF A :JOHN DOE - JR OF THE

FAMILY: BADY,WERE IN VIOLATION OF DUE PROCESS AND EQUAL PROTECTION OF

LAW BY PRESUMPTIONS. PRESUMPTIONS ARE A VIOLATION OF THE DUE PROCESS

CLAUSE IN THE 14TH AMENDMENT BY USING STATE LAWS WHICH VIOLATE THE

UNITED STATES CONSTITUTION, THE LAW OF THE LAND. THIS COURT'S RELIANCE

UPON ANY AND ALL PRESUMPTIONS IS A VIOLATION OF A :JOHN DOE - JR OF THE

FAMILY: BADY,RIGHT TO DUE PROCESS OF LAW.

DUE PROCESS OF LAW IS REQUIRED BEFORE THE DEPRIVATION OF LIFE, LIBERTY

AND PROPERTY. IT IS VERY IMPORTANT THAT DUE PROCESS OF LAW AND EQUAL

PROTECTION OF LAW IS FOLLOWED TO ENSURE THERE ARE NO CONCLUSIVE

PRESUMPTIONS BEING USED IN

THE DEPRIVATION OF A :JOHN DOE - JR OF THE FAMILY: BADY,LIFE, LIBERTY

AND PROPERTY.

THE UNITED STATES SUPREME COURT HAS HELD :JOHN DOE - JR OF THE FAMILY:

BADY, Y TIMES THAT PRESUMPTIONS CANNOT BE USED TO BYPASS CONSTITUTIONAL

GUARANTEES AS WELL AS PRESUMPTIONS BEING USED AS STEALTHY

ENCROACHMENTS UPON CONSTITUTIONAL RIGHTS OF A :JOHN DOE - JR OF THE

FAMILY: BADY REQUIRING THIS COURT TO MAINTAIN ITS :JOHN DOE - JR OF THE

FAMILY: BADY, DATE *OBSTA PRINICPIIS.* [*"It may be that it...is the obnoxious thing in its mildest*

and least repulsive form; but illegitimate and unconstitutional practices get their first footing in that way;

namely, by silent approaches and slight deviations from legal modes of procedure. This can only be

obviated by adhering to the rule that constitutional provisions for the security of person and property

should be liberally construed. A close and literal construction deprives them of half their efficacy, and leads *to gradual depreciation of the right, as if it consisted more in sound than in substance. It is the duty of the courts to be watchful for the constitutional rights of the citizens, and against any stealthy encroachments thereon. Their motto should be obsta prinicipiis," [***Mr. Justice Brewer, dissenting, quoting Mr. Justice Bradley in Boyd v. United***

States, 116 U.S. 616, 29 L.Ed. 746, 6 Sup.Ct.Rep. 524] [Hale v. Henkel, 201 U.S. 43 (1906)]]

I, :JOHN DOE - Jr of The Family: Bady, residing

In Idaho Republic is not a "sovereign citizen" nor a "constitutionalist" nor part of any cult or internet movement alleging laws do not apply, for he is of sound mind and body and recognizes laws consistent with the State of Idaho and United States Constitutions.

I, :JOHN DOE - Jr of The Family: Bady, hereby declares he has not waived his rights and he continues to stand upon these guaranteed inalienable rights protected by guaranteed due process of law and equal protection of laws under IDAHO and United States Constitutions, which all judicial actors must act and stand under, therefore this court and judicial actor is tasked with *obsta principiis* or he/she risks good behavior and shall be personally held for damages for trespass upon rights *cf. 42 USC sec 1983* and failure to cease and prevent further harm *cf. 42 USC Sec 1986* when a judge having the power and duty to do so, as the oath of office of a judicial actor is sworn to support and defend the United States Constitution or he/she forfeits judicial and qualified immunity under 11th amendment.

 The Supreme Court of the United States has held that judicial immunity is not presumed when a judicial actor comes into conflict with the superior power of the United States Constitution, the law of the land, whereby judicial immunity is not absolute in every matter before the court, it is presumed and presumptions must be proven by evidence introduced into the court.

This affidavit is de:JOHN DOE - Jr of The Family: Bady, ding to view the evidence introduced into court during evidentiary hearing resulting in granting this judicial or administrative entity the jurisdiction to create support orders ordering a third party Child Support Enforcement Agency to seize property, to suspend driving privileges, to suspend travel by freezing passport and to freeze bank accounts. Without evidence, all acting taken upon a :JOHN DOE - Jr of The Family: Bady, ;

are and were unlawful requiring the immediate discharge and dismissal of support orders and requiring this judicial actor and court to issue court orders ordering child support enforcement to cease and desist and order the immediate restoration of rights and property. **Definition of inalienable (adj.) Look up inalienable at Dictionary.com** *"that cannot be given up,"*

I, :JOHN DOE - Jr of The Family: Bady, hereby informs this court that he rebuts all conclusive presumptions therefore this court must not support use of presumptions without the clarification of evidence to support conclusive presumptions, such as obligor. An obligor is obligated to a contract, and proof of consent is required before calling a :JOHN DOE - Jr of The Family: Bady, obligor by providing proof he entered into a contract to pay child support through child support collection services. *obligor (n.)*

Look up obligor at Dictionary.com "person who binds himself to another by contract,"

The following child support terms are conclusive presumptions encroaching upon my rights to due process and equal protection of law.

I de:JOHN DOE - Jr of The Family: Bady, d these terms removed from any records unless this Title IV-D court can provide evidence it was authorized to use conclusive presumptions to assert guilt. *"The power to create presumptions is not a means of escape from constitutional restrictions."* [***Bailey v. Alabama, 219 U.S. 219 , 238, et seq., 31 S.Ct. 145; :JOHN DOE - Jr of The Family: Bady, ley v. Georgia, 279 U.S. 1 , 5-6, 49 S.Ct. 215***] 1. **Obligor;** The person obligated to pay child support (also referred to

as a noncustodial parent or NCP)

2. **Non-custodial parent**; the parent who does not have primary care, custody, or control of the child, and who may have an obligation to pay child support. Also referred to as the obligor.

3. **Biological Father;** The :JOHN DOE - Jr of The Family: Bady, who provided the paternal genes of a child. The biological father is sometimes referred to as the natural father.

4. **Payor;** Person who makes a payment, usually a noncustodial parent or someone acting on their behalf.

All Conclusive Presumptions by this Entity or Agent addressing this Judicial Review and De:JOHN DOE -

Jr of The Family: Bady, d for Dismissal and Discharge must be supported by Clarification of Evidence to Support Presumptions or the Presumptions will Prejudice or Injure the Protected Rights of the undersigned, a Violation of Due Process of Law that Results in a Void Judgment for failure to follow due process guaranteed by 5th and 14th amendments.

 The presumptions in this matter requiring evidence that due process of law and equal of protection of law were provided and presumption the undersigned is obligated by contract under Title IV-A to pay child support to

Title IV-D Child Support Collection contractor.
These presumptions must be proven by facts and evidence or this de:JOHN DOE - Jr of The Family: Bady, d for dismissal and discharge must be granted immediately without terms. **Black's Law Dictionary, Sixth Edition, defines "presumption" as follows:**

presumption. *An inference in favor of a particular fact. A presumption is a rule of law, statutory or judicial, by which finding of a basic fact gives rise to existence of presumed fact, until presumption is rebutted.* **Van Wart v. Cook, Okl.App., 557 P.2d. 1161, 1163.** *A legal device which operates in the absence of other proof to require that certain inferences be drawn from the available evidence.* **Port Terminal & Warehousing Co. v. John S. James 40 Co., D.C.Ga., 92 F.R.D. 100, 106.**

A "presumption" is not evidence, but simply a belief akin to a religion. *A presumption is an assumption of fact that the law requires to be made from another fact or group of facts found or otherwise established in the action. A presumption is not evidence. A presumption is either conclusive or rebuttable. Every rebuttable presumption is either (a) a presumption affecting the burden of producing evidence or (b) a presumption affecting the burden of proof. Calif.Evid.Code, §600.*

In all civil actions and proceedings not otherwise provided for by Act of Congress or by the Federal Rules of Evidence, a presumption imposes on the party against whom it is directed the burden of going forward with evidence to rebut or meet the presumption, but does not shift to such party the burden of proof in the sense of the risk of non persuasion, which remains throughout the trial upon the party on whom it was originally cast. Federal Evidence Rule 301.

See also Disputable presumption; inference; Juris et de jure; Presumptive evidence; Prima facie; Raise a presumption.

[Black's Law Dictionary, Sixth Edition, p. 1185]

Presumptions may not be imposed if they injure rights protected by the Constitution: A conclusive presumption may be defeated where its application would impair a party's constitutionally-protected liberty or property interests. In such cases, conclusive presumptions have been held to violate a party's due process and equal protection rights. [Vlandis v. Kline (1973) 412 U.S. 441, 449, 93 S.Ct. 2230, 2235; Cleveland Bed. of Ed. v.

LaFleur (1974) 414 U.S. 632, 639-640, 94 S.Ct. 1208, 1215-presumption under Illinois law that unmarried fathers are unfit violates process]

To implement the presumption, courts must be alert to factors that may undermine the fairness of the fact-finding process. In the administration of criminal justice, courts must carefully guard against dilution of the principle that guilt is to be established by probative evidence and beyond a reasonable doubt. In re Winship, 397 U.S. 358, 364 (1970). [425 U.S. 501, 504][Delo v. Lashely, 507 U.S. 272 (1993)]

1. **45 C.F.R. § 303.101(d)(2)** Evaluate evidence and make recommendations or decisions to establish paternity and to establish and enforce support orders. Whereas I understand it, there is no proof of paternity to establish support order.

  2. **45 C.F.R. § 303.101(d)(1)** Take testimony and establish a record. Whereas A :JOHN DOE - Jr of The Family: Bady, denies being afforded due process and equal protection of laws as required by 14th amendment, therefore these child support terms are presumptions insinuating guilt, which the facts and lack of physical evidence proves these presumptive terms are false therefore must be removed from all records claiming a Title IV-A child support loan was made to a :JOHN DOE - Jr of The Family: Bady, and this debt must be repaid to a IV-D State Collection Agency by income deduction or possible license suspension or incarceration may occur:

I, :JOHN DOE - Jr of The Family: Bady, is fully confident this court will protect against any stealthy encroachments upon these inalienable rights and will immediately dismiss and discharge this matter and will aid in the full restoration of property and vindication of rights deprived. I declare that a full discharge and dismissal for the unconstitutional procedures violating due process used in the efforts to collect an unsubstantiated debt for an unsubstantiated loan for public assistance under Title IV-A of the Social Security Act.

All state child support enforcement must be in accordance with federal child support enforcement under 45 CFR 303.101, therefore, I declare that a full discharge and dismissal for violation of the following 45 CFR 303.101 Expedited Processes requirements for which the presiding officer must:

1. 45 C.F.R. § 303.101(d)(2) Evaluate evidence and make recommendations or decisions to establish paternity and to establish and enforce support orders. Whereas I understand it, there is no proof of paternity to establish support order.

2. 45 C.F.R. § 303.101(d)(1) Take testimony and establish a record. Whereas a :JOHN DOE - Jr of The Family: Bady, denies being afforded due process and equal protection of laws as required by 14th amendment, therefore these child support terms are presumptions insinuating guilt, which the facts and lack of physical evidence proves these presumptive terms are false therefore must be removed from all records claiming a Title IV-A child support loan was made to a :JOHN DOE - Jr of The Family: Bady, and this debt must be repaid to a IV-D State Collection Agency by income deduction or possible license suspension or incarceration may occur: Whereas I understand it, there is no competent or expert witness testimony proving

JOHN DOE Bady Jr sired any offspring. 3. **45 C.F.R. § 303.101(d)(3)** Accept voluntary acknowledgments of paternity or support liability and agreements regarding the amount of support to be paid. Whereas I understand it, there is no evidence of

agreement for voluntary acknowledgement of paternity.

JOHN DOE Bady Jr denies any acknowledgement of paternity.

4. **Under 45 C.F.R. § 303.101(d)(3)** requires voluntary paternity testing to prove parentage, there is no record of paternity testing proving a :JOHN DOE - Jr of The Family: Bady, has sired any offspring. 5. **45 C.F.R. § 303.101(c)(2)** Parties must be afforded due process;

Whereas I understand it, the State of Idaho has seized property by denying my 14th amendment right to due process and equal protection of law and my property has been seized without a warrant in violation of the 4th amendment.

6. **45 C.F.R. § 303.101(c)(3)** Parties must receive copies of the order or paternity acknowledgment. Whereas I understand it, I have not received any paternity acknowledgement documents, and by this declaration refuses acknowledgement of paternity and refuses order for genetic testing.

The United States Department of Justice Civil Rights Division Memo dated March 16, 2016, stated the following:

1. *"Courts must safeguard against unconstitutional practices by court staff and private contractors."*

2. *"Courts must not use arrest warrants or license suspensions as a means of coercing the payment of court debt when individuals have not been afforded constitutionally adequate procedural protections."* Family Court and Child support enforcement contractors receives federal funds under Title IV-D 42 USC sec 658a for child support enforcement incentives, therefore has a pecuniary interest in the outcome of support proceedings, and this is a violation of the due process clause of the 14th amendment under Ward v Monroeville. ***Ward v. Village of Monroeville, Ohio, 409 U.S. 57, 61-62 (1972).***

*"In court systems receiving federal funds, these practices may also violate **Title VI of the Civil Rights Act of 1964, 42 U.S.C. § 2000d**, when they unnecessarily impose disparate harm on the basis of race or national origin".* *[DEPARTMENT OF JUSTICE CIVIL RIGHTS DIVISION MEMO DATED MARCH 16, 2016]*

Can this court support the practices by child support enforcement as constitutional? If it cannot, it must immediately dismiss and discharge with prejudice.

1. The due process and equal protection principles of the Fourteenth Amendment prohibit "punishing a person for his poverty." ***Bearden v. Georgia, 461 U.S. 660, 671 (1983).***

2. The Supreme Court recently reaffirmed this principle in ***Turner v. Rogers, 131 S. Ct. 2507 (2011)***, holding that a court violates due process when it finds a parent in civil contempt and jails the parent for failure to pay child support, without first inquiring into the parent's ability to pay. Id. at 2518-19.

3. To comply with this constitutional guarantee, state and local courts must inquire as to a

person's ability to pay prior to imposing incarceration for nonpayment.

Courts must not condition access to a judicial hearing on prepayment of fines or fees.

"State and local courts deprive indigent defendants of due process and equal protection if they condition

access to the courts on payment of fines or fees. ***See Boddie v. Connecticut, 401 U.S. 371, 374 (1971)***

(holding that due process bars states from conditioning access to compulsory judicial process on the

payment of court fees by those unable to pay); see also

Tucker v. City of Montgomery Bd. of Comm'rs, 410 F. Supp. 494, 502 (M.D. Ala. 1976) *(holding that*

the conditioning of an appeal on payment of a bond violates indigent prisoners' equal protection rights

and "'has no place in our heritage of Equal Justice Under Law'" ***(citing Burns v. Ohio, 360 U.S. 252,***

258 (1959))."

Suspending of drivers license is an unconstitutional administrative procedure by depriving a :JOHN

DOE - Jr of The Family: Bady, of his right to travel and hindering his livelihood and forcing further into

poverty. **Courts must not use arrest warrants or license suspensions as a means of coercing the**

payment of court debt when individuals have not been afforded constitutionally adequate

procedural protections. *"In :JOHN DOE - Jr of The Family: Bady, y jurisdictions, courts are also*

authorized—and in some cases required—to initiate the suspension of a defendant's driver's license to

compel the payment of outstanding court debts. If a defendant's driver's license is suspended because of

failure to pay a fine, such a suspension may be unlawful if the defendant was deprived of his due process

right to establish inability to pay. ***See Bell v. Burson, 402 U.S. 535, 539 (1971)*** *(holding that driver's*

licenses "may become essential in the pursuit of a livelihood" and

thus "are not to be taken away without that procedural due process required by the Fourteenth

Amendment"); ***cf. Dixon v. Love, 431 U.S. 105, 113-14 (1977)*** *(upholding revocation of driver's license*

after conviction based in part on the due process provided in the underlying criminal proceedings);

Mackey v. Montrym, 443 U.S. 1, 13-17 (1979) *(upholding suspension of driver's license after arrest for*

driving under the influence and refusal to take a breath-analysis test, because suspension "substantially

served" the government's interest in public safety and was based on "objective facts either within the

personal knowledge of an impartial government official or readily ascertainable by him," making the

risk of erroneous deprivation low). Accordingly, automatic license suspensions premised on determinations that fail to comport with Bearden and its progeny may violate due process."

[DEPARTMENT OF JUSTICE CIVIL RIGHTS DIVISION MEMO DATED MARCH 16, 2016] **Courts must safeguard against unconstitutional practices by court staff and private contractors.**

Under 42 USC section 658a Title IV-d Child Support Enforcement incentive payments results in the child support enforcement contractor

having a significant pecuniary interest in the outcome, and as in this matter, will use expedited processes to speed up the process so the state of Idaho can receive these federal funds at the cost of a :JOHN DOE - Jr of The Family: Bady, rights to due process and equal protection of laws guaranteed under the 14th amendment. This court was created to provide remedy and equal protection of laws pursuant the symbol of a blindfolded wo:JOHN DOE - Jr of The Family: Bady, holding a scale, therefore it is required that this court must guard against these encroachments.

"Additional due process concerns arise when these designees have a direct pecuniary interest in the :JOHN DOE - Jr of The Family: Bady, agement or outcome of a case—for example, when a jurisdiction employs private, for-profit companies to supervise probationers. In :JOHN DOE - Jr of The Family: Bady, y such jurisdictions, probation companies are authorized not only to collect court fines, but also to impose an array of discretionary surcharges (such as supervision fees, late fees, drug testing fees, etc.) to be paid to the company itself rather than to the court. Thus, the probation company that decides what services or sanctions to impose stands to profit from those very decisions. The Supreme Court has "always been sensitive to the possibility that important actors in the criminal justice system may be influenced by factors that threaten to compromise the

perfor:JOHN DOE - Jr of The Family: Bady, ce of their duty." **Young v. U.S. ex rel. Vuitton et Fils S.A., 481 U.S. 787, 810 (1987)**. *It has expressly prohibited arrangements in which the judge might have a pecuniary interest, direct or indirect, in the outcome of a case. See* **Tumey v. Ohio, 273 U.S. 510, 523 (1927)** *(invalidating conviction on the basis of $12 fee paid to the mayor only upon conviction in mayor's court);* **Ward v. Village of Monroeville, Ohio, 409 U.S. 57, 61-62 (1972)** *(extending reasoning of Tumey to cases in which the judge has a clear but not direct interest). It has applied the same reasoning to prosecutors, holding that the appointment of a private prosecutor with a pecuniary interest in the outcome of a case constitutes fundamental error because it "undermines confidence in the integrity of the criminal proceeding." Young, 481 U.S. at 811-14. The appointment of a private probation company with a* *pecuniary interest in the outcome of its cases raises similarly fundamental concerns about fairness and due process"* [DEPARTMENT OF JUSTICE CIVIL RIGHTS DIVISION MEMO DATED MARCH 16, 2016]

THE FOLLOWING CAN BE FOUND IN CHAPTER 6 Essentials for Attorneys in Child Enforcement EXPEDITED JUDICIAL AND ADMINISTRATIVE PROCESSES

Constitutionality

The movement from judicial processes for CSE to administrative processes has raised issues of constitutionality. These are generally issues of separation of powers and due process.

Separation of Powers *The separation of powers issue raised by the advent of administrative processes is whether the legislature can delegate a traditionally judicial area to the Executive branch of Government. The answer depends, in large part, on State constitutional law. Generally, State legislatures have broad authority to determine the right and responsibilities of citizens and to establish processes for enforcing those responsibilities. PRWORA did not :JOHN DOE - Jr of The Family: Bady, date the administrative establishment of child support orders, leaving the decision as to whether to remove this function from the Judicial branch and place it with the Executive branch up to the States. The Supreme Court of Minnesota recently held the administrative child support process created by its legislature to be a violation of the separation of powers doctrine.*

Minnesota's administrative process included procedures for uncontested and contested cases. In uncontested cases, the agency prepared a proposed support order for the parties' signature and the administrative law judge's ratification. If either party contested the proposed order, the case moved into the contested process. In the contested process, the case was presented by a child support officer (CSO) who was not an attorney. The administrative law judge (ALJ) had judicial powers, including the ability to modify judicial child support orders. While the ALJ could not preside over contested paternity and contempt proceedings, he or she could grant stipulated contempt orders and uncontested paternity orders. While recognizing the importance of streamlining child support mechanisms, the Minnesota Supreme Court stated it could not ignore separation of powers constraints. It concluded that the administrative structure violated separation of powers for three reasons. First, the administrative process infringed on the district court's jurisdiction in contravention to the Minnesota Constitution. Second, ALJ jurisdiction was not inferior to the district court's jurisdiction, as :JOHN DOE - Jr of The

Family: Bady, dated by the Minnesota Constitution. Third, the administrative process empowered non-

attorneys to engage in the practice of law, infringing on the court's exclusive power to supervise the

practice of law. The decision was stayed for several months to give the legislature time to amend

Minnesota laws in accord with the decision. **Due Process**

The question of due process raises a fundamental Federal constitutional protection. The 14th

Amendment to the United States Constitution provides

22

that a person "shall not be deprived of life, liberty, or property without due process of law." The U.S.

Supreme Court has established some very important criteria for due process, falling into three general

areas: Challenges have arisen to the :JOHN DOE - Jr of The Family: Bady, ner in which administrative

process is invoked. An illustrative case is Holmberg v. Holmberg, in which the Minnesota Supreme Court

held that the State's administrative process for child support orders was unconstitutional. The legislature

had put into place a system under which uncontested child support cases could be heard by administrative

law judges, who had the power to set child support awards, and to modify awards previously set by circuit

courts. The orders were directly appealable to the appellate court, without review by the district court. The

Minnesota Supreme Court held that such a system is unconstitutional because it violates the separation of

powers doctrine and usurps the original jurisdiction of the district court.

[http://www.acf.hhs.gov/sites/default/files/programs/css/essentials_for_attor neys_ch06.pdf]

One or more of the constitutional safeguards has been violated in the expedited processes for

assessment of support and issuance of an alleged support order alleging a debt exists for a loan under

Title IV-A of Social

23

Security Act. The court must provide proof of a money judgment entered with county clerk pursuant All

Writs Section proving that all writs coming from a court within the US must have a clerk's signature

pursuant 28 USC section 1691 or it is void .

The Court hearing this de:JOHN DOE - Jr of The Family: Bady, d for dismissal and discharge has the

judicial responsibility to ensure the equal protection clause provided the 14th amendment protecting against any state child support laws and administrative procedures which shall violate the following:

1. The 14th amendment protection from State Laws and administrative procedures which shall violate

inalienable rights guaranteed in the state and US Bill of Rights. *A fundamental, constitutional*

guarantee that all legal proceedings will be fair and that one will be given notice of the

proceedings and an opportunity to be heard before the government acts to take away one's life,

liberty, or property. Also, a constitutional guarantee that a law shall not be unreasonable,

Arbitrary, or capricious

   http://legal-dictionary.thefreedictionary.com/due+process+of+law 2. 7th Amendment Right

to a trial by jury in controversies of $20 or more.

24

3. The threat of incarceration must allow for right to counsel in accordance with 6th
   amendment.

4. The 4th amendment guarantee of freedom from seizure of property unless by due process of

law by a warrant with oath or affirmation. The seizure of property were violated and this

court must guard against violation . All courts are created for remedy and this declaration

and de:JOHN DOE - Jr of The Family: Bady, d for remedy by issuance of dismissal and

discharge with prejudice.

I, :JOHN DOE - Jr of The Family: Bady, is confident this Court will immediately dismiss and

discharge this matter with prejudice. Thank you. **CERTIFICATION**

The undersigned hereby affirms under threat of perjury that the aforementioned affidavit is true and the

information in italics were accumulated from *45 CFR 303.101*, *Chapter 6 Essentials for Attorneys*

Health and Hu:JOHN DOE - Jr of The Family: Bady, Services and *United States Department of*

Justice Civil Rights Division dated March 16, 2016.

FURTHER AFFIANT SAITH NOT.
Subscribed and sworn, without prejudice, and with all rights reserved,
Printed Name:) **:JOHN DOE - Jr of The Family: Bady**,
Principal, by Special Appearance, proceeding Sui Juris.

Signed:_____

Date:_____

On this_____day of_____,_____, before me, the undersigned, a Notary Public in and for_____, personally appeared the above-signed, known to me to be the one whose name is signed on this instrument, and has acknowledged to me that s/he has executed the same.

Signed:_____

Printed Name:_____

Date:_____

Address:_____

CASE NUMBER: CVDR0700994
EXHIBIT _____

LETTER ROGATORY FOR RELIEF

Under the Hague Convention Title 18 §1781

I, **:JOHN DOE - Jr of The Family: Bady**, a living Soul and breathing Man and Executor for the **JOHN DOE BADY JR** Cestui que trust, notice the Court of my Letter Rogatory to the **IDAHO COURTS** and demand my name be cleared of this alleged family court case for the reasons set forth below:

1) I, **:JOHN DOE - Jr of The Family: Bady** have learned that this alleged Court that has scheduled a case/cause/claim against me is not really a court as per the Constitution of the United States of America (not an Article III Court), but rather a military tribunal under Admiralty jurisdiction and is operated as a private, for profit corporation listed on Dun and Bradstreet.

2) I have learned of the fraud that goes on behind the scenes of these alleged criminal cases, which are really civil claims in equity, and the steps taken to securitize these civil claims, without giving full disclosure to the people. I am hereby letting the court know that I am opting out of any contract and do not allow any documents regarding me or my cestui que trust to be securitized and sold to investors etc.

3) As you may be fully aware, the fraudulent process is as follows: All cases are civil, though often fraudulently called criminal. The courts are operating under trust law, assuming the Defendant and Respondent is a decedent (civiliter mortus). After finding the alleged Defendant guilty, the court clerks sell the judgments to the Federal Courts. Since the Defendant and or Respondent is a decedent, presumed to be a ward of the court, incompetent and of unsound mind, the court officials consider themselves as a beneficiary as the powers that be (international bankers) have concocted a reverse trust scheme on we, the people, who are supposed to be the beneficiaries because we are the actual creditors.

4) When a judge asks if a person understands, he/she is asking if the person is liable for the bond. I am not responsible for the bond of this/these cases, but I will appoint the Judge as Trustee/Fiduciary and be the beneficiary of all proceeds.

5) The judgments are stamped with something to the effect of Pay To The Order Of_on the back and taken to the federal discount window. The judgment now becomes a note

6) The notes are then pooled together and then become securities, which are yet to be pooled together and sold as bonds.

7) Said bonds are liens against me, a defendant-in-error.

8) The United States Attorney's Office has a put code number, NAICS (North American Identification Security Classification. Said NAICS number enables the United States Attorney's Office to trade globally all securities.

9) All US federal courts are registered with the DOD (Department of Defense), where they are registered with CCR (Contractor's Central Registration), under the DOD, which another department called DLIS

1

(Defense Logistics Information Service), which issues a cage code, which means a commercial and government entity, which everything corresponds with their bank account.

10) Said United States Attorney's Office and the Courts have a Duns number (Dun & Bradstreet).

11) Everything filed into court is securitized without the knowledge or consent of the people or of all parties involved.

12) All criminal cases not heard in an Article 3 court (District Court of the United States) are actually civil; however, the courts again commit fraud by labeling the case as criminal, even for an infraction as minimal as a parking ticket. All cases which are plead out or have a guilty conviction label the civil defendants (through unlawful conversion) as felons when they are not. This is a fraud upon the people at large, and certainly fraud upon the alleged Defendants-in-error.

13) The Bank Account is at the Federal Reserve Bank of New York, in New York City. The Depository Agreement is signed by the Clerk of Court.

14) All securities are then deposited with the DTC in New York.

15) An Escrow Agent is used as a go-between - between the Clerk's Office and the Federal Reserve Bank of New York.

16) The securities end up being listed through the Seventh Circuit (Chicago, IL), then sent to the DTCC, the clearinghouse whom lists the securities for trading.

17) All of the lawyers involved are acting as private debt collectors according to the **FDCPA (Title 15§1692).** The BAR Association exempts them from having to be registered as such; however, they operate through call warrants, which are like a put, or a call. Doing margin calls is where they convert a case through (similar to a Writ of Execution) use the case number to buy equity securities.

18) Everything filed into court is securitized and turned into negotiable instruments, and then turning them into securities. These items are sold commercial items, calling them distress debts (Unifund). The items are then pooled together in what is now called a hedge fund, where they are sold globally.

19) Anytime when there is risk management involved, it is for the securities. This is an underwriting company. When the hedge funds are going into the global market, they go through Luer Hermes, a bond holder and underwriting company and subdivision of Alliance SE, of Munich ,Germany (Pimco Bonds).

20) After 9 months, all paper is converted to a securities status. This is defined in **Title 15§77(a)(b)(1)** and is now considered to be an investment contract. The paper is endorsed to become a security, and the trust is then collapsed.

21) The courts have an account with the IMF (International Monetary Fund) under Interpol. The Judges involved and the US Attorneys involved do not have an accessible Oath of Office , because they cover up the fact that the oath of office is between them and the IMF.

22) The US Judges and US Attorneys are actually employees of the IMF and have expatriated out of the United States. They are now unregistered foreign agents under **Title 22**, which states all foreign agents must be registered. These hypocrites don't even adhere to their own codes.

23) The court judgments are deposited with the IMF. Since this case obviously involves me, I have a drawing to all proceeds. See **UCC §3-305 and §3-306**. The court judgments are monopolized according to **Title 16**, which is a violation of antitrust laws, and also unfair trade practice.

24) Indictments are True Bills, meaning they are negotiable instruments. The District Attorney failed to give me a 1099 OID showing me as the recipient of the funds, which is a fraud upon me. In my case, I have not been indicted, but still request a 1099 OID, unless the court wishes to close this account.

25) The unlawful funds, through fraud and deception, are deposited in the Federal Reserve Bank of New York and they have not paid the tax on this income. According to the IRC, this is a **§7201** of **Title 26** violation (willful failure to file with the intent to evade the tax).

26) A copy of the Depository Resolution Agreement was not made available to me from the Clerk of Court. The Clerk of Court makes deposits into the Federal Reserve Bank of New York via electronic funds transfers (EFT's).

27) The Clerk has a PMIA (Private Money Investment Account) is, which also has a government code. According to Clerks Praxis, the Clerk of the US District Court is the Registrar in Admiralty.

28) According to the **IRS §6209** Decoding Manual and the ADP (Automated Data Processing Manual), all 1099's are Class 5 gift and estate taxes. I am asking for a 1099 OID in this case, as I am not willing to gift you the proceeds. I am hereby asking for the proceeds in their entirety, including interest.

29) It is presumed that by the creation of the birth certificate, my body the labor there from is pledged to the State. This is patently absurd as this unilateral, quasi-contract is lacking in full disclosure to the parents and the babies still in their cribs.I have never pledged my rights nor my body, any labor thereof, nor any creation therefrom to any gifting program, including any court or court process.

30) I am not a charitable organization. I demand all funds from the cases (current and past cases) be sent to me within 30 days or I will file complaints to the IRS and SEC explaining the fraud and theft committed upon me, and issue a 1099 OID.

31) I demand my name and my cestui que trust name, **JOHN DOE BADY JR** be removed from any and all government databases indicating bad credit, commercial liens and/or the titles of criminal, felon and/or debtor be removed immediately and permanently NUNC PRO TUNC.

32) I hereby request a copy of the Depository Resolution Agreement from the Clerk of Court. And a W-9 from the Judge and the US Attorney involved, if you wish to proceed with this case.

33) I hereby notice the Court that I am the Executor of the cestui que trust of **JOHN DOE BADY JR**. According to **Title 26 §303 & §7701**, companies, corporations, and associations and trusts are all decedents. This means my all capital letters name is a legal estate. My all capital letters name falls into this class. I direct all of the affairs and financial affairs of **JOHN DOE BADY JR**, an Estate.

3

34) I demand this case/account be closed and no further steps taken to securitize it.

35) I hereby ask the Court, as my fiduciary and trustee, to notify local agents and agencies to put me on a do not disturb or detain list so that we do not have to go through this again. Additionally, I demand compensation from the **STATE OF IDAHO** in the amount of **$10,000.00** for the commercial injury I have sustained from the loss of my property, loss of time from work, the cost of certified mailings of **AFFIDAVITS, NOTICE AND DEMAND** letters to the parties involved, the cost of filings and recordings as well as the expenses incurred for traveling as a result of being deprived of the use of my private property (automobile) which was unlawfully converted for public use.

36) I want to remain confident that the Court and its officers want to follow the law, and perhaps were unaware of the processes of civil and criminal cases and that the public policy enforcers are ignorant of the aforementioned facts regarding their often erroneous administration of the Cestui que trust.

37) I expect no further harassment from rogue unregistered foreign agents and public policy enforcers acting under color of law.

LETTER ROGATORY FOR RELIEF

FURTHER AFFIANT SAITH NOT.

Subscribed and sworn, without prejudice, and with all rights reserved,

(Printed Name:) **:JOHN DOE - Jr of The Family: Bady,**

Principal, by Special Appearance, proceeding Sui Juris.

Signed:_____

Date:_____

On this_____day of_____,_____, before me, the undersigned, a Notary Public in and for _____, personally appeared the above-signed, known to me to be the one whose name is signed on this instrument, and has acknowledged to me that s/he has executed the same.

Signed:_____

Printed Name:_____

Date:_____

Address:_____

4

NOTICE OF MISTAKE

1. **TAKE NOTICE THAT:** In the matter of SURETY for the **JOHN DOE BADY JR**, I believe that there has been a MISTAKE, as the SOLE BENEFICIARY OF A PUBLIC DOCUMENT has been INCORRECTLY IDENTIFIED as an "accused" and/or a "suspect".
2. **FORGIVE ME:** If I, AND/OR PERSONS AND/OR FRIENDS OF THE COURT AND/OR SUCH OTHER PARTIES ACTING IN MY INTERESTS, have led A COURT and/or STATUTORY BODY and/or A GOVERNMENT SERVICE and/or AGENTS and/or OFFICERS of such bodies, to believe, by responding to "You", and/or "**JOHN DOE BADY JR**", and/or SUCH OTHER IDENTIFICATION, such bodies HAVE ADDRESSED ME AS, that I am the PARTY WITH SURETY in this matter, then that would be a MISTAKE, and please forgive me.
3. If I, AND/OR PERSONS AND/OR FRIENDS OF THE COURT AND/OR SUCH OTHER PARTIES ACTING IN MY INTERESTS, have led A COURT and/or STATUTORY BODY and/or A GOVERNMENT SERVICE and/or AGENTS and/or OFFICERS of such bodies, to believe, by responding to "You", and/or "**JOHN DOE BADY JR**" and/or SUCH OTHER IDENTIFICATION, such bodies HAVE ADDRESSED ME AS, that I am, in ANY CAPACITY, a *Pro Se* litigant and/or a LEGAL PERSON in this matter, then that would be a MISTAKE, as I DO NOT CONSENT and WAIVE THE BENEFIT to such titles (Waiver of the CHANGE OF NAMES ACT OF FEDERAL RULES), and please forgive me.
4. **THEREFORE:** As I have no knowledge of who "You" and or "**JOHN DOE BADY JR**" and/or SUCH OTHER IDENTIFICATION ANY COURT and/or STATUTORY BODY and/or GOVERNMENT SERVICE and/or AGENTS and/or OFFICERS of such bodies [HEREAFTER "YOU"], HAS ADDRESSED ME AS, I RESPECTFULLY ASK; by WHAT AUTHORITY ARE "YOU" ADDRESSING me as such?
5. As the SURETY BOND (BIRTH CERTIFICATE) has been deposited into the COURT [*In the custody of JOHN DOE G. Wasden*], WHAT EVIDENCE does the COURT have that I, as aMAN who is not lawfully entitled to the BENEFITS of a BIRTH CERTIFICATE, have any SURETY in this matter?
6. As GOVERNMENT is the SOLE SIGNATORY PARTY on the SURETY BOND (BIRTH CERTIFICATE), with SOLE AND FULL SURETY as TRUSTEE for the LEGAL NAME, WHAT EVIDENCE do YOU have that I am a TRUSTEE for the LEGAL NAME. WHAT EVIDENCE do YOU have that I am a TRUSTEE and have ANY SURETY with respect to ANY NAME?
7. WHAT EVIDENCE do YOU have, that I am an OFFICER, an AGENT, a TRUSTEE and/or an EMPLOYEE of the CROWN? WHAT EVIDENCE do "YOU" have of any WARRANT OF AGENCY for the principal?
8. WHAT EVIDENCE do "YOU" have that there has been any meeting of the minds, any PROPER NOTICE given, any considerable CONSIDERATION offered, or that I have ANY INTENT to CONTRACT in this matter?

As such, I am returning your OFFER, DECLINED, for immediate DISCHARGE and CLOSURE.

DEMAND TO RELEASE LEIN OF GARNISHMENT OF WAGES AND STATEMENT OF FACTS

I DEMAND TO COLLAPSE TRUST AND RELEASE GARNISHMENT OF PAYROLL WAGES.

<u>EXPARTE DAVIS, 344 SW 2d 925 (1976)</u> : Federal statutes guarantee protection (to the Respondent) from having "imputed income" orders. Furthermore, these statutes provide (to the Respondent) protection of his rights to be free from unlawful child support or any kind of garnishment. That, child support is a civil matter and there is no probable cause to seek or issue body attachment, bench warrant, or arrest in child support matters because it is a civil matter.

The use of such instruments (body attachment, bench warrants, arrests, Including garnishment of waages etc.) presumably is a method to "streamline" arresting people for child support and circumventing the Fourth Amendment to the United States Constitution, and is used as a debt-collecting tool using unlawful arrests and imprisonment to collect a debt or perceived debt.

The arrest of non-custodial parents in which men make up significant majority of the "arrestees", is "gender profiling", "gender biased discrimination" and a "gender biased hate crime" in that it violates the Equal Protection Clause of the Fourteenth Amendment. A man, pursuant to the Equal Protection Clause of the Constitution of the United States, cannot be arrested in a civil matter as a woman is not. There is no escaping the fact that there is no probable cause in a civil matter to arrest or issue body attachment. "Probable cause" to arrest requires a showing that both a crime has been, or is being committed, and that the person sought to be arrested committed the offense. U.S.C.A. Const. Amend. 4. In the instant case, no probable cause can exist, because the entire matter has arisen out of a civil case. Therefore, seeking of body attachment, bench warrant, or arrest by the Petitioner (and her attorney), and/or issuing of the same by the court, in this civil case would be against the law and the Constitution.

Under **U.S. v. Rylander** ignorance of the order or the inability to comply with the child support order, or as in this case, to pay, would be a complete defense to any contempt sanction, violation of a court order or violation of litigant's rights.

Every U.S. Court of Appeals that has addressed this issue, has held that child support is a common, commercial (and civil) debt, See, U.S. v. Lewko, 269 F.3d 64, 68-69 (1st Cir. 2001)(citations omitted) and U.S. v. Parker, 108 F.3d 28, 31 (3rd Cir. 1997). Allen v. City of Portland, 73 F.3d 232 (9th Cir. 1995), the Ninth Circuit Court of Appeals (citing cases from the U.S. Supreme Court, Fifth, Seventh, Eighth and Ninth Circuits) "by definition, probable cause to arrest can only exist in relation to criminal conduct; civil disputes cannot give rise to probable cause"; Paff v.

Kaltenbach, 204 F.3d 425, 435 (3rd Cir. 2000) (Fourth Amendment prohibits law enforcement officers from arresting citizens without probable cause. See, Illinois v. Gates, 462 U.S. 213 (1983), therefore, no body attachment, bench warrant or arrest order may be issued.

If a person is arrested on less than probable cause, the United States Supreme Court has long recognized that the aggrieved party has a cause of action under 42 U.S.C. §1983 for violation of Fourth Amendment rights. Pierson v. Ray, 386 U.S. 547, 87 S.Ct. 1213 (1967). Harlow v. Fitzgerald, 457 U.S. 800, 818 (there can be no objective reasonableness where officials violate clearly established constitutional rights such as--(a) United States Constitution, Fourth Amendment (including Warrants Clause), Fifth Amendment (Due Process and Equal Protection), Ninth Amendment (Rights to Privacy and Liberty), Fourteenth Amendment (Due Process and Equal Protection).

Child Support is a fictitious debt created by fraud and deception. Child Support is a Title IV-D collection agency for TANF Block Grants. A grant is something granted and gifted nothing tied to a debt or debt collections, In the International Covenant on Civil and Political Rights Article 1 Section 2 clearly states the following: All peoples may, for their own ends, freely dispose of their natural wealth and resources without prejudice.

Trinsey v Pagliaro, D.C.Pa. 1964, 229 F.Supp. 647.

It's a VIOLATION of the 11th Amendment for a FOREIGN CITIZEN to INVOKE the JUDICIAL POWER of the State.

Article XI.

The Judicial power of the United States shall not be construed to extend to any suit in law or equity, commenced or prosecuted against one of the United States by Citizens of another State, or by Citizens or Subjects of any Foreign State.

"An attorney for the plaintiff cannot admit evidence into the court. He is either an attorney or a witness".

(Trinsey v. Pagliaro D.C.Pa. 1964, 229 F. Supp. 647)

US citizens (FEDERAL CITIZENS) are FOREIGN to the several States and SUBJECTS of the FEDERAL UNITED STATES/STATE of NEW COLUMBIA/DISTRICT OF COLUMBIA.

Attorneys are considered FOREIGN AGENTS under the FOREIGN AGENTS REGISTRATION ACT (FARA) and are SUBJECTS of the BAR ASSOCIATION.

NOTICE OF DEMAND OF OATH OF OFFICE and STATEMENT OF JURISDICTION

PUBLIC NOTICE FOR:

d/b/a: Special Deputy Attorney – **Robert Vail (Individual Capacity) & (official capacity) State of Idaho**

and Court Clerks, sundry employees, officers, agents, et al.

a/k/a: PUBLIC SERVANTSs – **State of Idaho**

NOTICE TO PRINCIPAL IS NOTICE TO AGENT
NOTICE TO AGENT IS NOTICE TO PRINCIPAL

Point of Law

All contracts commence with an offer and only become binding upon acceptance. See Farnsworth on Contracts ©2004 by E. Allan Farnsworth, Third Edition, Aspen Publisher, ISBN: 0-7355-4605-3 (Vol. 1) 3.3

The People's Contract a/k/a "The Constitution of the United States of America" or "This Constitution" (Articles 1-6; Bill of Rights 1-10) mandates an oath of office for all officers in public service to wit: " . . . the judges in every State shall be bound thereby, any Thing in the Constitution or Laws of an State to the Contrary notwithanding."

Further, the CONSTITUTION OF THE STATE OF IDAHO mandates every PERSON elected or appointed subscribe to an oath that he will "support"[1] and "maintain" the Constitution for the United States and the constitution of "this state," (20.1) and purchase a faithful performance bond as a good faith pledge that the Officer will conduct his/her duties per the requirements of both constitutions "before entering upon his duties" in relation to his/her public office as a PUBLIC SERVANT (22.19; NMSA 7-2-2 thru 7-2-7).

BE IT KNOWN that . . . from the beginning, with the Lord Jesus Christ as my Witness, I, Stephan D Mattox, "grateful to Almighty God for the blessings of liberty," repent of all my transgressions against my King, Lawgiver, and Judge; and, with faith in His saving grace, waive all claims without my Creator.

BE IT KNOWN to **ROBERT VAIL** AND ALL COURT OFFICIALS AND ATTORNEYS et al. that I accept your oath(s) of office d/b/as "Judge" or "other" for the State of **Idaho** provided that you are competent to conduct the duties of office having subscribed to the required oath and posted a faithful performance bond as required by fundamental law.

FURTHERMORE NOTICES *all custodians of the public trust* to *release all* custodial holding[s] completely leaving no residue being held by any custodian whatsoever and return all property or interest either tangible, intangible, *ledger*[financial] and real property in this matter as I am the sole surviving heir of my parent's precious and lawful love, and have the only absolute claim of dominion.

Should the above statements not be true, then let the record be corrected or it will stand as truth.

All rights Reserved,

[1] *Support*, n. 5. In general, the *__maintenance__* or sustaining of any thing *__without suffering it to fail, decline or languish.__* Daniel Webster's Dictionary (1828). [Emphasis added]

Maintain, v.t. [L. manus and teneo.] 1. To hold, preserve or keep in any state or condition; to support; to sustain; not suffer to fail or decline. Daniel Webster's Dictionary (1828).

I hereby give you ten (10) days to reply to this notice from the above date with a notice sent using recorded post and signed under full commercial liability and penalties of perjury, assuring and promising me that all of the replies and details given to the above requests are true and without deception, fraud or mischief. Your said failure to provide the aforementioned documentation within ten (10) days, from the above date, to validate the debt, will constitute your agreement to the following terms:

That the debt did not exist in the first place;
OR
It has already been paid in full;
AND
That any damages suffer, you will be held culpable;
That any negative remarks made to a credit reference agency will be removed;
You will no longer pursue this matter any further.
You agree to pay all fee schedules.

Please Note: I wish to deal with this matter in writing and I do not give your organization permission to contact me by telephone. Should you do so, I must warn you that the calls could constitute 'harassment' and I may take action under Section 1 of the Protection from Harassment Act 1997 and the Administration of Justice Act 1970 S.40, which makes it a Criminal Offence for a creditor or a creditor's agent to make demands (for money), which are aimed at causing 'alarm, distress or humiliation', because of their frequency or manner.

STATMENT OF FACTS

__For the record we wish to effect payment immediately. What is the sum certain on the penal funds?__

Affiant is a national *of the nation/state of Idaho, as contemplated by the act of congress evidenced and restated at* **8 U.S.C. 1101(a)(2).** *Affiant is aware and knows that the U.S. bankruptcy is verified in* **Senate Report No. 93-519 93rd. Congress, 1st Session (1973), Summary of Emergency Power Statues, "Executive Orders 6073, 6102, 6111, and by Executive Order 6260 on March 9th, 1933 under the "Trading with the Enemy Act (Sixty-Fifth Congress, Session 1, Chapters 105, 106, October 6th, 1917, and as further codified at 12 U.S.C.A. 95(a) and (b)** *as amended.*

- I conditionally accept all facts in the claim if the respondent can prove authority to make presentments
- I conditionally accept for value and return for value the presumption I have a duty to show cause for actions upon proof of claim that it is not public policy of the **UNITED STATES** under **HJR-192** *to not pay debts at law but instead to exchange consideration upon a dollar for dollar basis to discharge or offset a liability.*
- I conditionally accept for value and return for value the presumption I have a duty to show cause for my actions with the bank or respondent upon proof of claim that without money of account (*as established under* **Article One, Sections 10,** *clause one, of the Organic Constitution of the Untied States of America*) in circulation that the only commercial consideration that exists is each and every person's exemption by way of a prepaid account operated by the United States Secretary of Treasury.

Affiant is aware and knows that a certificate of live birth (certificate of title) is a bond that evidences title held by the **Depositary Trust Company (DTCC).** The issuer has legal title; you have equitable title up until you partner up to share equitable title with the United States. SS-5 creates the UPPERCASE NAME which is surety for the Vessel. The Vessel is the body and evidenced on the application by length, weight, and footprints. A body manifested into the sea of commerce. The beneficiary is supposed to be Me, Myself, and I. But the Depositary Trust Company (DTCC) is at 55 Water Street New York City and operates both the public and the private side. Under Civil Rico Racketeering Laws **18 U.S.C.** 1964 as corporations may have established a pattern of racketeering activity by using mail to collect an unlawful debt. If proven there is a conspiracy to deprive of property without due process is various constitutional injuries under **18 U.S.C.A. 241.** *Knowledge and neglect to prevent a United States Constitutional wrong.* **31 U.S.C. 5118 (d)2 None can ask for payment in specific coin. 31 U.S.C. 3123** There is no money, so no one can demand payment... the United States will discharge debt dollar for dollar.

Affiant is aware and knows that legal tender (FEDERAL RESERVE NOTES) are not good and lawful money of the United States. See Rains V. State,State, 226 S.W .18

Affiant is aware and knows that the Undersigned affiant has been estopped from using and has no access to ' lawful Constitutional Money of exchange' (see U.S. Constitution- Article 1 Section 10) to "pay debts at law", and pursuant to HJR-192, can only discharge fines, fees, debts, and judgements 'dollar for dollar' via commercial paper or upon Affiant's Exemption.

There are no judicial courts in America and there has no been since 1789. Judges do no enforce statutes and codes. Executive Administrators enforce statutes and codes. (FRC V. GE 281 US464 KELLER V. PE 261 US 428, 1 STAT. 138-178

I HEREBY notice that I am the executor of the Cestui Que Vie Trust of **JOHN DOE BADY JR** according to Title 26 sections 303 & 7701, companies, corporations, and associations and trusts are all decedents. This means my all UPPERCASE NAME IS A LEGAL ESTATE. My ALL UPPERCASE NAME falls into this class. I direct all of the affairs and financial affairs of **JOHN DOE BADY JR**

The following documents are needed to move forward in these matters
All tax bond receipts 1099 OID, 1099A, 1099C

The authorization from the INTERNAL REVENUE SERVICE to go forward with the above mentioned account number [26 U.S.C. 2032A(e)11]
Employee Affidavit [Title 5 U.S.C. 3333]
Registration [Title 22 U.S.C. 611 and 612]

Please provide all of the following information and submit the appropriate forms and paperwork back to me along with an affidavit signed in accordance with 28 U.S.C. 1746 for validation and proof of claim.

I affirm that all statement, facts, and information presented in this affidavit/ writ are correct and are presented as evidence for the record. Evidence, exhibit, Information, and facts are placed in Evidence in this case, and As I am reserving and retaining all my rights and affirm to the best of my knowledge and belief.

MAY ALL PARTIES BE MINDFUL OF 48 CFR, 48 U.S.C., UNIFORM COMMERICAL CODES 1-308, 3-402, 3-419 3-501,

Affiant is aware and know that the various and numerous references to case law, legislative history, state and federal statutes/ codes, Federal Reserve Bank Publications, Supreme Court decisions, the Uniform Commercial Codes, U.S. Organic Constitutional, and general recognized maxims of Law as cited herein and throughout establish the following:

A) That the U.S. Federal government and the several United States did totally and completely debase the organic Lawful Constitutional Coin of the several States of the Union of the United States.
B) That the Federal Government and the several United States have and continue to breach the express mandates of Article 1 Section 10 of the Federal Constitution regarding the minting and circulation of lawful coin.
C) That the lawful coin (i.e. organic medium of exchange) and the former ability to PAY DEBTS has been replaced with fiat, paper currency, with the limited capacity to only discharge debts.

D) That Congress of the United States did legislate and provide the American People a remedy/ means to discharge all debt "dollar for dollar" via HJR-192 due to the declared Bankruptcy of the Corporate United States via the abolishment of Constitutional Coin and Currency.
No Assured value, no liability, errors, nor omissions excepted. All rights reserved and retain without recourse-non-assumpsit

FURTHER AFFIANT SAITH NOT.

Subscribed and sworn, without prejudice, and with all rights reserved,
(Printed Name:) **JOHN DOE**   of the family name **Brady**

Principal, by Special Appearance, proceeding Sui Juris.

Signed:_____
Date:_____

On this_____day of_____,_____, before me, the undersigned, a Notary Public in and for _____, personally appeared the above-signed, known to me to be the one whose name is signed on this instrument, and has acknowledged to me that s/he has executed the same.

Signed:_____
Printed Name:_____
Date:_____
Address:_____

AFFIDAVIT OF FACTS
JOHN DOE BADY JR'S SPECIAL DEMURRER

:JOHN DOE- Jr of The Family: Bady NUNC PRO TUNC assertsallher unalienable rights, privilegesand immunities at Natural Law, Common Law and Maritime Law, and all her commercial rights relevant to this state.

Special Appearance
:JOHN DOE- Jr of The Family: Bady asserts his special appearance, objecting to the court's subject matter jurisdiction, personal jurisdiction, and venue.

Objection to Non-Judicial Decision-makers
:JOHN DOE- Jr of The Family: Bady objects to, does not consent to, and affirmatively withholds all consent regarding, the assignment of this case, in any part, to any decision-maker who is not a "judge" (1) who has been properly elected or appointed and (2) who has an active oath of office. *Cf. Gonzalez v. United States*, **U.S. (12 May 2008)** ("If the parties consent").

Special Demurrer
:JOHN DOE- Jr of The Family: Bady *moves and demands for dismissal of each and every "charge and cause."*

Discussion
General Demurrer is incorporated by reference.
:JOHN DOE- Jr of The Family: Bady continues her objections to this court's exercise of subject matter jurisdiction, personal jurisdiction, and venue, as discussed in his General Demurrer.
Due Process Affidavit and Brief is incorporated by reference.
:JOHN DOE- Jr of The Family: Bady continues her objections to the horrific Due Process problems inherent in this case, as discussed in her Due Process Affidavit and Brief.
Non-waiver of Arraignment document is incorporated by reference.
:JOHN DOE- Jr of The Family: Bady recognizes the court's good faith effort into getting newly discovered evidence on and for the Record, and for reasons beyond the court's control,
:JOHN DOE- Jr of The Family: Bady still objects to Notice in this case, these cases. Moreover, should STATE opt against dismissal and in favor of amendment, the Arraignment sequence will start all over, again.

What is STATE OF IDAHO?
Since **STATE OF IDAHO** has an **EIN No.**, it follows that **STATE OF IDAHO** is a commercial entity.
If **STATE OF IDAHO** were independently "sovereign," it would be beholden to nothing, and its "citizens" would not be paying "taxes" to anything except the state "sovereign" system acting as agent for those people. Where **STATE OF IDAHO** does not "defend" its "citizens" from/against "tax" claims of another commercial entity/system, it follows that **STATE OF IDAHO** is a commercial subsidiary of that other commercial system.
Moreover, it's impossible to have a legitimate governmental system where there is no legitimate Money in general circulation. Thus, where there is no gold or silver Coin in general circulation, and where what passes as "legal tender" does so solely because it is so labeled, it

follows that the system that tolerates that "funny money" scam, evidenced by the prosecution of no one who runs that "funny money" scam, is a commercial system. Still further, that "funny money"-based system operates not per the Law of the Land, but rather per the Law of the Sea. Only in this legal environment may the "funny money" scam remain unprosecuted. That legal environment is that of a "Constitution-free, maritime, commercial zone." What is **STATE OF IDAHO**? It's a commercial entity operating commercially, via a tax exemption certificate, in a Constitution-free, maritime, commercial zone called "this state."

Notice of Special Appearance by Affidavit
Challenge of jurisdiction under **Title 5 USC 556(d)**-[burden of proof is on the government.]
Quaelibet Jurisdictio Cancellos Suos Habet
*'Every jurisdiction has its own limits.' **Jenk. Cent. Cas. 139.***

"A special appearance is an appearance solely for the purpose of testing the jurisdiction."
Bailey v. Schrada, 34 Ind. 261; Huff v. Shepard, 58 Mo. 246

A special appearance is for the purpose of testing the sufficiency of service or the jurisdiction of the court;
State v. Huller, 23 N.M. 306, 168 P. 528, 534, 1 A.L.R. 170.

COMES NOW RESPONDENT/AFFIANT, **:JOHN DOE- Jr of The Family: Bady,** herein after called "Respondent", in pro per, sui juris, NOT a pro se party with this Affidavit of Special Appearance. Respondent is appearing before this court Specially, and not Generally, in Pro Per ("in one's own proper person"), Sui Juris, regarding above trust number,

This Special Appearance by Affidavit is for the purposes of challenging the courts presumption and assumption of jurisdiction

I hereby declare, reserve, claim and retain ALL rights and defects in process. I claim and reserve all of my rights under **UCC 1-308**. I further declare that I am a Man and living soul and NOT a 'legal fiction' I am not a member of the political or legal society over which the court has jurisdiction, and I do not agree to be characterized as a legal fiction. I revoke all powers of attorney past and present *nunc pro tunc* as I am competent to handle my own affairs.

I, **:JOHN DOE- Jr of The Family: Bady,** am a living Man and living soul. Is there a man or woman who has a claim against me?

1. Challenge Negates Jurisdiction
By this Affidavit, Affiant challenges the subject-matter and in personam jurisdiction of this court. Therefore, this court now is without jurisdiction.

The presumption that officials have done their duty is limited by the rule that a presumption cannot be based upon a mere presumption, and will not supply proof of independent, substantive facts, such as that a deficiency judgment was entered and docketed by the clerk of the court. " **Mahoney v Boise Title & T. Co.** 1926) 116 Okla 202, 244 P 170

Once jurisdiction is challenged, the court cannot proceed when it clearly appears that the court lacks jurisdiction, the court has no authority to reach merits, but rather, should dismiss the action. **Melo v. US, 505 F2d 1026.**

"Once jurisdiction is challenged it must be proven." **Hagans v. Levine 415 US 533 note 3**

The law requires proof of jurisdiction to appear on the record of the administrative agency and all administrative proceedings." **Hagans v Lavine, 415 U. S. 533.**

"No sanction can be imposed absent proof of jurisdiction."**Stanard v. Olesen, 74 S.Ct. 768**

"The law provides that once State / Federal Jurisdiction has been challenged, it must be proven." **Maine v. Thiboutot, 100 S. Ct. 2502 (1980)**

"Once challenged, jurisdiction cannot be assumed, it must be proved to exist." **Stuck v. Medical Examiners, 94 CA2d 751.211 P2s 389**

"The burden shifts to the court to prove jurisdiction." **Rosemond v. Lambert, 469 F2d 416.**

"Court must prove on the record, all jurisdiction facts related to the jurisdiction asserted." **Lantana v. Hopper, 102 F. 2d 188; Chicago v. New York 37 F Supp. 150**

Jurisdiction, once challenged, is to be proven, not by the court, but by the party attempting to assert jurisdiction. The burden of proof of jurisdiction lies with the asserter. The court is only to rule on the sufficiency of the proof tendered. **McNutt v. GMAC, 298 US 178. Origins found in Maxfield's Lessee v Levy, 4 US 308**

"It is impossible to prove jurisdiction exists absent a substantial nexus with the state such as voluntary subscription to license. All jurisdictional facts supporting claim that supposed jurisdiction exists must appear on the record of the court."**Pipe Line v. Marathon. 102 S. Ct. 3858 quoting Crowell v. Benson 883 US 22**

"Therefore, it is necessary that the record present the fact establishing the jurisdiction of the tribunal" **Lowe v. Alexander 15C 296; People v. Board of Delegates of S.F. Fire Dept 14 C 279**

2. Jurisdiction Not Within Discretion of Court
Affiant reminds this court that the matter of jurisdiction is not a matter within the discretion of this court. "A court has no jurisdiction to determine its own jurisdiction, for a basic issue in any case before a tribunal is its power to act, and a court must have the authority to decide that question in the first instance." **Rescue Army v. Municipal Court of Los Angeles, 171 P2d 8; 331 US 549, 91 L. ed. 1666, 67 S.Ct. 1409.**

A court "generally may not rule on the merits of a case without first determining that it has jurisdiction over the category of claim in the suit (subject-matter jurisdiction) . . . ." **Sinochem Int'l Co. Ltd. v. Malaysia Int'l Shipping Corp., 549 U.S. 422, 430–31 (2007)**

"The burden shifts to the court to prove jurisdiction." **Rosemond v. Lambert, 469 F2d 416.**

"The proponent of the rule has the burden of proof.."**Title 5 U.S.C. §556(d)**

3. Jurisdiction Cannot Be Waived
The principles of waiver, consent, and estoppel do not apply to jurisdictional issues—the actions of the litigants cannot vest a district court with jurisdiction above the limitations provided by the Constitution and Congress. "If the record does not show upon its face the facts necessary to give jurisdiction, they will be

presumed not to have existed." **Norman v. Zieber, 3 Orat202-03**

4. Jurisdiction Can Be Raised At Any time
Federal Rule 12(h)(3) states that, "f the court determines at any time that it lacks subject-matter jurisdiction, the court must dismiss the action." **Fed. R. Civ. P. 12(h)(3).**

"Jurisdiction can be challenged at any time." and "Jurisdiction, once challenged, cannot be assumed and must be decided." **Basso v. Utah Power & Light Co., 495 F2d 906, 910.**

"Defense of lack of jurisdiction over the subject matter may be raised at any time, even on appeal." **Hill Top Developers v. Holiday Pines Service Corp., 478 So. 2d. 368 (Fla 2nd DCA 1985)**

"The objection that a federal court lacks subject-matter jurisdiction may be raised by a party, or by a court on its own initiative, at any stage in the litigation, even after trial and the entry of judgment." **Arbaugh v. Y & H Corp., 546 U.S. 500, 506 (2006) (citations omitted) (jurisdiction upheld); see also Kontrick v. Ryan, 540 U.S. 443, 455 (2004)**

On appeal—even for the first time at the Supreme Court—a party may attack jurisdiction after the entry of judgment in the district court. **Arbaugh v. Y & H Corp., 546 U.S. 500, 514 (2006).**

Even the party that had invoked the district court's jurisdiction can argue on appeal, to avoid an adverse judgment, that the district court lacked jurisdiction. **13 Wright & Miller § 3522, pp. 122–23**

'Where the question of jurisdiction in the court of the person, the subject matter, or the place where the crime was committed can be raised, in any stage of a criminal proceeding; it is never presumed, but must always be proved; and it is never waved by the respondent." **U.S. v. Rogers, District Court Ark.,23 Fed 58 1855**

5. Acts by Court a Nullity
Affiant notices this court that any action taken by the court absent proof of is a nullity.
A universal principle as old as the law is that a proceedings of a court without jurisdiction are a nullity and ts judgment therein without effect either on person or property." **Norwood v. Renfield, 34 C 329; Ex parte Giambonini, 49 P. 732.**

Where there is absence of jurisdiction, all administrative and judicial proceedings are a nullity and confer no right, offer no protection, and afford no justification, and may be rejected upon direct collateral attack." **Thompson v. Tolmie, 2 Pet. 157, 7 L.Ed. 381; Griffith v. Frazier, 8 Cr. 9, 3L. Ed. 471.**

Jurisdiction is fundamental and a judgment rendered by a court that does not have jurisdiction to hear is oid ab initio." **In Re Application of Wyatt, 300 P. 132; Re Cavitt, 118 P2d 846.**

Thus, where a judicial tribunal has no jurisdiction of the subject matter on which it assumes to act, its roceedings are absolutely void in the fullest sense of the term." **Dillon v. Dillon, 187 P 27.**

: *LACK OF JURISDICTION*: No witness, no facts, no jurisdiction.
There is no discretion to ignore lack of jurisdiction." **Joyce v. U.S., 474 F2d 215.**

No sanction can be imposed absent proof of jurisdiction." "Once challenged, jurisdiction cannot be assumed'; it must be proved to exist!" **Stanard v. Olesen, 74 S.Ct. 768**

"Thus, where a judicial tribunal has no jurisdiction of the subject matter on which it assumes to act, its proceedings are absolutely void in the fullest sense of the term." **Dillon v. Dillon, 187 P 27.**

In regard to courts of inferior jurisdiction, "if the record does not show upon its face the facts necessary to give jurisdiction, they will be presumed not to have existed." **Norman v. Zieber, 3 Or at 202-03**

"Where a person is not at the time a licensee, neither the agency, nor any official has any jurisdiction of said person to consider or make any order. One ground as to want of jurisdiction was, accused was not a licensee and it was not claimed that he was."**O'Neil v. Dept Prof. & Vocations 7 CA 2d 398; Eiseman v. Daugherty 6 CA 783**

"A court cannot confer jurisdiction where none existed and cannot make a void proceeding valid. It is clear and well established law that a void order can be challenged in any court" **OLD WAYNE MUT. L. ASSOC. v. McDONOUGH, 204 U. S. 8, 27 S. Ct. 236 (1907).**

"Court must prove on the record, all jurisdiction facts related to the jurisdiction asserted. **"Latana v. Hopper, 102 F. 2d 188; Chicago v. New York 37 F Supp. 150**

"Where the question of jurisdiction in the court of the person, the subject matter, or the place where the crime was committed can be raised, in any stage of a criminal proceeding; it is never presumed, but must always be proved; and it is never waved by the respondent." **U.S. v. Rogers, District Court Ark.,23 Fed 658 1855**

"Therefore, it is necessary that the record present the fact establishing the jurisdiction of the tribunal" **Lowe v. Alexander 15C 296; People v. Board of Delegates of S.F. Fire Dept 14 C 279**

"It is basic in our law that an administrative agency may act only within the area of jurisdiction marked out for it by law. If an individual does not come within the coverage of the particular agency's enabling legislation the agency is without power to take any action which affects him." **Endicott v. Perkins, 317 US 501**

"If the court is not in the exercise of its general jurisdiction, but of some special statutory jurisdiction, it is as to such preceding an inferior court, and not aided by presumption in favor of jurisdiction." **1 Smith's Leading Cases, 816**

"Inferior courts" are those whose jurisdiction is limited and special and whose proceedings are not according to the course of the common law." **Ex Parte Kearny, 55 Cal. 212; Smith v. Andrews, 6 Cal. 652**

JURISDICTION

I am here by way of Special Appearance to challenge jurisdiction and to have this matter dismissed. I believe this court lacks jurisdiction.

1. I want to see the jurisdiction duly placed into evidence. In the copy of the file I have it is nonexistent.

2. I don't believe this court can produce a competent witness against me.

3. I don't believe this court can produce lawful oath of office for judge.

4. I don't believe this court has a valid cause of action against me nor was there proper due process.

5. I don't believe this court has any evidence against me

This court must prove jurisdiction.

WHEREAS, Affiant demands this court for dismissal of this action and release/removal and collapse the above trust number(s) without prejudice along with just compensation for injuries caused and time invested for preparing lawful documents in this matter made payable immediately to Affiant in the amount of **$5000**.

VERIFICATION

Under the penalty of perjury of the laws of the **State of IDAHO** , I, **JOHN DOEBADY JR** , depose, declare, certify, verify, and state, that I am at least 21 years of age, that I am competent to make this Verification, and that the statements of fact are within my personal knowledge, and that the statements of law are within my best efforts and to the best of my understanding and belief.

The statements in this document are true and correct. Key, for all times relevant to this matter, these matters, I have never acted or intended to act within any concept of "transportation." I am not in the "transportation" business, and I have had, and still have, no desire to be in the "transportation" business.

For all times relevant to this matter, I have never remotely had any intent to remove people and/or goods from here to there for profit or hire under any choice of law, much less the choice of law of the place called "this state."

For all times relevant to this matter, I was intentionally and knowingly "traveling," and that under a choice of law of the Law of the Land. Further, Declarant sayeth not.

FURTHER AFFIANT SAITH NOT.

Subscribed and sworn, without prejudice, and with all rights reserved,
Printed Name:) :JOHN DOE- Jr of The Family: Bady
Principal, by Special Appearance, proceeding Sui Juris.

Signed:_____
Date:_____

On this_____day of_____,_____, before me, the undersigned, a Notary Public in and for_____, personally appeared the above-signed, known to me to be the one whose name is signed on this instrument, and has acknowledged to me that s/he has executed the same.

Signed:_____
Printed Name:_____
Date:_____
Address:_____

THE HONORABLE COURTS OF IDAHO

AFFIDAVIT

DEMAND TO DISMISS

Affiant, :JOHN DOE- JR OF THE FAMILY: BADY., sui juris, a common man of the Republic People, does swear and affirm that Affiant has scribed and read the foregoing facts, and in accordance with the best of Affiant's firsthand knowledge and conviction, such are true, correct, complete, and not misleading, the truth, the whole truth, and nothing but the truth.

JOHN DOE BADY JR

VS

CVDR0700994

STATE OF IDAHO

ROBERT VAIL (SPECIAL DEPUTY ATTORNEY)

DEMAND to DISMISS

JOHN DOE Bady Jr Demands to move the court to dismiss this case for the following reasons.

1. THE RESERVATION OF MY RIGHTS.

JOHN DOE- JR OF THE FAMILY: BADY, explicitly reserve all of my rights. UCC 1-308 which was formally UCC 1-207.

1-308. Performance or Acceptance Under Reservation of Rights.

a) A party that with explicit reservation of rights performs or promises erformance or assents to performance in a manner demanded or offered by the other party does not thereby prejudice the rights reserved. Such words as "without prejudice," "under protest," or the like are sufficient.

2. FURTHER ADVISEMENT

This is to advise that all of the actions of the court and all others in these cases against JOHN DOE BADY JR are in violation of ...

A. USC TITLE 18 > PART I > CHAPTER 13 > § 242 Deprivation of rights under color of law

B. USC TITLE 18 > PART I > CHAPTER 13 > § 241 Conspiracy against rights

WHEREFORE, :JOHN DOE- JR OF THE FAMILY: BADY, demands and prays for the foregoing speedy relief.

Kindest and warmest regards,

Signed_____
Without prejudice UCC 1-308
:JOHN DOE- JR OF THE FAMILY: BADY,

Notification of reservation of rights
UCC1-308/UCC 1-207

PUBLIC
Your name here, :JOHN DOE- JR OF THE FAMILY: BADY, sui juris

THIS IS A PUBLIC COMMUNICATION TO ALL
UCC1-308

Notice to agents is notice to principles
Your Address
Notice to principles is Notice to Agents
Your Address
Applications to all successors and assigns
Your Address
All are without excuse

Let it be known to all that I, your name here explicitly reserves all of my rights.
UCC1-308 which was formally UCC 1-207.
Further, let all be advised that all actions commenced against me may be in
violation of,...
USC TITLE 18 > PARTI > CHAPTER 13 > § 242 Deprivation of rights under color of
law
USC TITLE 18 > PARTI > CHAPTER 13 > § 241 Conspiracy against rights
Wherefore all have undeniable knowledge.

Signed_____sui juris,
This Affidavit is dated_____.

NOTARY PUBLIC
STATE OF COUNTY OF_____

Subscribed and sworn to before me, a Notary Public, the above signed your name
here.

This day of_____, 2021
Notary Public

MY COMMISSION EXPIRES:_____

CASE NUMBER: 123-YOUR-CASE-NUMBER
EXHIBIT _____

Certified Mail #_____

Mailed by: Jeffery Wayne McBride Jr
              Trust

1101 E CUMBERLAND AVE STE 201H

TAMPA, FLORIDA 33602

To: Cathlene Robinson   NOTICE TO AGENT IS NOTICE TO PRINCIPAL
              D/b/a Court Clerk   NOTICE TO PRINCIPAL IS NOTICE TO AGENT

              c/o Fulton County
              Superior
              Courthouse

              136 Pryor St SW
              Atlanta, Georgia
              [30303]

Date: _____

Re: complaint on case 21CP200858   JEFFERY WAYNE MCBRIDE JR

Notice of Acceptance

    Please be advised that I have accepted your presentment to JEFFERY WAYNE MCBRIDE JR
for assessed value and am returning it to you in exchange for closure and settlement to account #
21CP200858.
Please send the confirmation that the account for case # 21CP200858 has been adjusted and
settled,to the address shown above, or send a notice of dishonor from a qualified third party.
I am also enclosing an authorization for you to facilitate the use of my credit to discharge all
court charges that may apply. The instructions and statement of account are attached for your
convenience.

    Your refusal to send the confirmation or notice of dishonor will in no way negate this
settlement, and will be your agreement that you and your agency have no capacity to pursue
collection, further collection efforts confirm your agreement that you and your agency,
collectively and severably owe JEFFERY WAYNE MCBRIDE JR $25,000, and the
JEFFERY WAYNE MCBRIDE JR may take all necessary steps to secure its claim to the
debt owed to it and to collect.

Thank you for your immediate attention to this matter.

                                    Sincerely,

                                    _____
No: 9898   Jeffery Wayne McBride Jr.

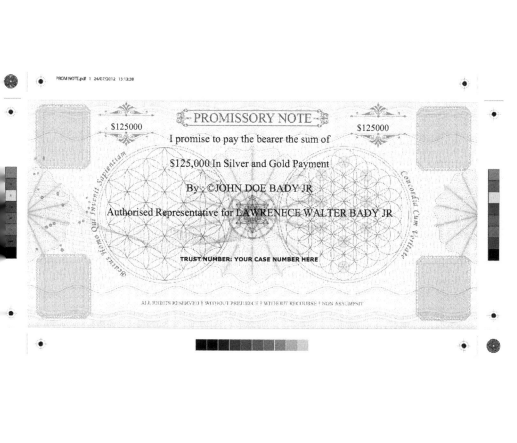

PROMISSORY NOTE

$125000

$125000

I promise to pay the bearer the sum of

$125,000 In Silver and Gold Payment

By: ©JOHN DOE BADY JR

Authorised Representative for LAWRENECE WALTER BADY JR

TRUST NUMBER: YOUR CASE NUMBER HERE

LETTER OF EVIDENCE OF TAX-EXEMPT FOREIGN STATUS

For the purposes of this Letter of Evidence the terms "United States" and "U.S." mean only the Federal Legislative Democracy of the District of Columbia, Puerto Rico, U.S. Virgin Islands, Guam, American Samoa, and any other Territory within the "United States," which entity has its origin and jurisdiction from Article I Section 8, Clause 17-18 and Article IV, Section 3, Clause 2 of the Constitution of the United States of America. The terms "United States" and "U.S." are NOT to be construed to mean or include the sovereign, united 50 states of America.

1. I was neither born nor naturalized in the United States, nor "subject to its jurisdiction, therefore I am NOT and never have been, as described in 26 CFR 1.1-1(c) and the 14th Amendment, a "U.S. citizen." Therefore, I am an "alien" with respect to the "United States."

2. I am NOT and never have been, as described in 26 USC 865(g)(1)(A), a "resident of the "U.S."

3. I have NEVER made, with ANY "knowingly intelligent acts" (Brady v. U.S. 397 U.S. 742, 748), ANY voluntary election under 26 USC 6013 or 26 CFR 1.871-4 to be treated as a "U.S. resident alien" for any purpose. Further, I have utterly NO intention of making such election in the future.

4. I AM, as described in 26 USC 865(g) (1) (B), a "nonresident alien" of the "United States."

5. I am NOT and never have been as described in 26 USC 7701(a)(30), a "U.S. person."

6. I am NOT and never have been, as described in 26 USC 7701(a) (14), a "taxpayer."

7. I do NOT have and never have had, as described in 26 USC 911(d)(3), a "tax home within the U.S."

8. I AM therefore, as described in 26 CFR 1.871-2 and 26 USC 770l(b), a "non-resident alien" with respect to the "United States" and am outside the general venue and jurisdiction of the "U.S."

9. I am NOT and never have been, as described in 26 USC 3401, an "officer" or an "employee" or an "elected official" (of the "United States" or of a "State" or of any political subdivision thereof, nor the District of Columbia, nor of a "domestic" corporation) earning wages from an "employer."

10. I am NOT and never have been, as described in 31 USC 3713, a "fiduciary," or as described in 26 USC 6901, a "transferee" or a "transferee of a transferee."
Form AFD-01 Secured Party: Andrew Lee Leo Hill, ALLH Nonadverse Party Page 2 of 3

11. I am NOT and never have been, as described in 26 USC Subtitle B, a "donor" or a "contributor," and as a "nonresident alien" excluded under' 26 USC 2501(a) (2), therefore, I AM EXEMPT from any gift tax under 26 USC Subtitle B.

12. As a "non-resident alien" NOT engaged in or connected with any "trade or business within the United States," I am NOT REQUIRED by law to obtain a "U.S." Taxpayer Identification Number or Social Security Number because of my exemption under 26 CFR 301.6109-1 (g). Further, I AM NOT REQUIRED by law to make, as described in 26 CFR 1.6015(a)-1, a "declaration," because I am exempt under 26 CFR 1.6015(i)-1 and fundamental law.

13. As a "nonresident alien," I have NO "self employment income," as described in 26 CFR 1.1.1402 (9b)-3(d).

14. As a "nonresident alien," I derived NO gross income from sources within the "United States" either "effectively connected" or "not effectively connected" with the conduct of a trade or business in the "United States" as described in 26 USC 872{a}.

15. As a "nonresident alien," my private-sector remuneration is "from sources without the "United States" as described in 26 CFR 1.1441-3(a), does NOT constitute 26 USC 3401 "wages," and is therefore NOT "subject to" mandatory withholding under 26 USC 3402(a), 3101(a), or 26 CFR 1.1441-1, because of its EXEMPTION under 26 USC 3401(a)(6) and fundamental law.

16. As a "nonresident alien," I did NEVER intentionally make, with ANY knowingly intelligent acts, ANY voluntary withholding "agreement" as described in 26 USC 3402(p).

17. As a "nonresident alien," my income is NOT included in "gross income" under Subtitle A and is EXEMPT' from withholding according to 26 CFR 1.44l-3(a) and 26 CFR 31.340l(a)(6)-1(b).

18. As a "nonresident alien" with NO income "from sources within the United States," my private-sector, non-"U.S." income is FREE from all federal tax under fundamental law (see Treasury Decisions 3146 and 3640, and United States v. Morris 125 F. Rept 322, 331).

19. As a "nonresident alien," my estate and/or trust is, as described in 26 USC 7701 (a) (31), a TAX-EXEMPT "foreign estate or trust."

20. As a "natural born Citizen" (II:I:5 of the Constitution), free Sovereign, American Citizen, and "nonresident alien" with respect to the federal "United States," I did NEVER voluntarily, intentionally waive, with ANY "knowingly intelligent acts," ANY of my unalienable rights, and I have utterly NO intention of doing so in the future. Form AFD-01 Secured Party: Andrew Lee Leo Hill, ALLH Nonadverse Party Page 3 of 3 Any prima facie evidence and SSA forms, statements, etc. were in error and involuntarily made under threat, duress, and/or coercion. I hereby revoke, cancel, and render void, Nunc Pro Tunc, both currently and retroactively to the time of signing, any and all such signatures. I reserve the right NOT to be compelled to perform under any agreement that I have not entered into knowingly, voluntarily, and intentionally.

21. I am NOT a 26 USC 7203 "person required"; I am a "non-taxpayer" outside both general and tangential venue and jurisdiction of Title 26, United States Code.

Pursuant to 28 USC 1746(1) and executed "without the United States," I believe and affirm under penalty of perjury under the Laws of the United States of America that the foregoing is true and correct, to the best of my belief and informed knowledge. Subscribed, sealed, and affirmed to this day, 14th, month, September, and year of 2017 I hereby affix my own signature to all of the above affirmations with explicit reservation of ALL my unalienable rights and without prejudice to ANY of those rights (UCC 1-308).
* NOTICE TO THE AGENT IS NOTICE TO THE PRINCIPAL *
* NOTICE TO THE PRINCIPAL IS NOTICE'TO THE AGENT *

_____Jeffery Wayne McBride Jr
First Witness Matt. 18:16 Authorizing Representative for Secured Party
UCC 1-103 as per §§ 45.05.006

Honorably,
™ Jeffery: Wayne- of the family: McBride ©, Secured Party and Creditor

Jeffery Wayne McBride Jr,
c/o 1101 E Cumberland Ave Ste 201H-108
Tampa, Florida [33602]
    RepublicUnited States
zip code exempt (DMM 122.32)

Authorized Signature: DEBTOR_____

Autograph & Seal By: Secured Party Creditor_____
WITHOUT PREJUDICE-WITHOUT RECOURSE-NON-ASSUMPSIT
All Rights Reserved-Errors & Omissions Excepted

Dated:_____Day of_____, 2021

Notary Public's Signature: _____

Notary Public's Seal

Form **W-8BEN**

(Rev. July 2017)

Department of the Treasury
Internal Revenue Service

Certificate of Foreign Status of Beneficial Owner for United States Tax Withholding and Reporting (Individuals)

▶ For use by individuals. Entities must use Form W-8BEN-E.
▶ Go to *www.irs.gov/FormW8BEN* for instructions and the latest information.
▶ Give this form to the withholding agent or payer. Do not send to the IRS.

OMB No. 1545-1621

Do NOT use this form if: Instead, use Form:

- You are NOT an individual W-8BEN-E
- You are a U.S. citizen or other U.S. person, including a resident alien individual W-9
- You are a beneficial owner claiming that income is effectively connected with the conduct of trade or business within the U.S.
  (other than personal services) W-8ECI
- You are a beneficial owner who is receiving compensation for personal services performed in the United States . . . . . . 8233 or W-4
- You are a person acting as an intermediary W-8IMY

Note: If you are resident in a FATCA partner jurisdiction (i.e., a Model 1 IGA jurisdiction with reciprocity), certain tax account information may be provided to your jurisdiction of residence.

Part I Identification of Beneficial Owner (see instructions)

1 Name of individual who is the beneficial owner

John Henry Doe

2 Country of citizenship

American National

3 Permanent residence address (street, apt. or suite no., or rural route). Do not use a P.O. box or in-care-of address.

home address

City or town, state or province. Include postal code where appropriate.

City, State [zip]

Country

united States of America

4 Mailing address (if different from above)

City or town, state or province. Include postal code where appropriate.

Country

5 U.S. taxpayer identification number (SSN or ITIN), if required (see instructions)

N/A See: CLAIMANT of FOREIGN STATUS and

6 Foreign tax identifying number (see instructions)

N/A

7 Reference number(s) (see instructions)

N/A

8 Date of birth (MM-DD-YYYY) (see instructions)

CLAIMANT of TAX-EXEMPT FOREIGN STATUS N/A

Part II Claim of Tax Treaty Benefits (for chapter 3 purposes only) (see instructions)

9 I certify that the beneficial owner is a resident of _____ within the meaning of the income tax treaty between the United States and that country.

10 **Special rates and conditions** (if applicable—see instructions): The beneficial owner is claiming the provisions of Article and paragraph _____ of the treaty identified on line 9 above to claim a _____ % rate of withholding on (specify type of income): _____

Explain the additional conditions in the Article and paragraph the beneficial owner meets to be eligible for the rate of withholding: _____

Part III Certification

Under penalties of perjury, I declare that I have examined the information on this form and to the best of my knowledge and belief it is true, correct, and complete. I further certify under penalties of perjury that:

- I am the individual that is the beneficial owner (or am authorized to sign for the individual that is the beneficial owner) of all the income to which this form relates or am using this form to document myself for chapter 4 purposes,
- The person named on line 1 of this form is not a U.S. person,
- The income to which this form relates is:
  (a) not effectively connected with the conduct of a trade or business in the United States,
  (b) effectively connected but is not subject to tax under an applicable income tax treaty, or
  (c) the partner's share of a partnership's effectively connected income,
- The person named on line 1 of this form is a resident of the treaty country listed on line 9 of the form (if any) within the meaning of the income tax treaty between the United States and that country, and
- For broker transactions or barter exchanges, the beneficial owner is an exempt foreign person as defined in the instructions.

Furthermore, I authorize this form to be provided to any withholding agent that has control, receipt, or custody of the income of which I am the beneficial owner or any withholding agent that can disburse or make payments of the income of which I am the beneficial owner. I agree that I will submit a new form within 30 days if any certification made on this form becomes incorrect.

Sign Here ▶

Date

Signature of beneficial owner (or individual authorized to sign for beneficial owner)

Sign Last, First, Middle

Date (MM-DD-YYYY)

Doe, John, Henry

Print name of signer

Capacity in which acting (if form is not signed by beneficial owner)

For Paperwork Reduction Act Notice, see separate instructions.   Cat. No. 25047Z   Form **W-8BEN** (Rev. 7-2017)

Form **W-9**
(Rev. October 2018)
Department of the Treasury
Internal Revenue Service

Request for Taxpayer
Identification Number and Certification

▶ Go to *www.irs.gov/FormW9* for instructions and the latest information.

Give Form to the
requester. Do not
send to the IRS.

Print or type.
See Specific Instructions on page 3.

1 Name (as shown on your income tax return). Name is required on this line; do not leave this line blank.

2 Business name/disregarded entity name, if different from above

3 Check appropriate box for federal tax classification of the person whose name is entered on line 1. Check only **one** of the following seven boxes.

☐ Individual/sole proprietor or single-member LLC ☐ C Corporation ☐ S Corporation ☐ Partnership ☐ Trust/estate

☐ Limited liability company. Enter the tax classification (C=C corporation, S=S corporation, P=Partnership) ▶ _____

Note: Check the appropriate box in the line above for the tax classification of the single-member owner. Do not check LLC if the LLC is classified as a single-member LLC that is disregarded from the owner unless the owner of the LLC is another LLC that is **not** disregarded from the owner for U.S. federal tax purposes. Otherwise, a single-member LLC that is disregarded from the owner should check the appropriate box for the tax classification of its owner.

☐ Other (see instructions) ▶

4 Exemptions (codes apply only to certain entities, not individuals; see instructions on page 3):

Exempt payee code (if any) _____

Exemption from FATCA reporting code (if any) _____

Applies to accounts maintained outside the U.S.

5 Address (number, street, and apt. or suite no.) See instructions.

Requester's name and address (optional)

6 City, state, and ZIP code

7 List account number(s) here (optional)

Part I   Taxpayer Identification Number (TIN)

Enter your TIN in the appropriate box. The TIN provided must match the name given on line 1 to avoid backup withholding. For individuals, this is generally your social security number (SSN). However, for a resident alien, sole proprietor, or disregarded entity, see the instructions for Part I, later. For other entities, it is your employer identification number (EIN). If you do not have a number, see *How to get a TIN*, later.

Note: If the account is in more than one name, see the instructions for line 1. Also see *What Name and Number To Give the Requester* for guidelines on whose number to enter.

Social security number

☐☐☐ – ☐☐ – ☐☐☐☐

or

Employer identification number

☐☐ – ☐☐☐☐☐☐☐

Part II   Certification

Under penalties of perjury, I certify that:

1. The number shown on this form is my correct taxpayer identification number (or I am waiting for a number to be issued to me); and
2. I am not subject to backup withholding because: (a) I am exempt from backup withholding, or (b) I have not been notified by the Internal Revenue Service (IRS) that I am subject to backup withholding as a result of a failure to report all interest or dividends, or (c) the IRS has notified me that I am no longer subject to backup withholding; and
3. I am a U.S. citizen or other U.S. person (defined below); and
4. The FATCA code(s) entered on this form (if any) indicating that I am exempt from FATCA reporting is correct.

Certification instructions. You must cross out item 2 above if you have been notified by the IRS that you are currently subject to backup withholding because you have failed to report all interest and dividends on your tax return. For real estate transactions, item 2 does not apply. For mortgage interest paid, acquisition or abandonment of secured property, cancellation of debt, contributions to an individual retirement arrangement (IRA), and generally, payments other than interest and dividends, you are not required to sign the certification, but you must provide your correct TIN. See the instructions for Part II, later.

Sign Here   Signature of U.S. person ▶   Date ▶

General Instructions

Section references are to the Internal Revenue Code unless otherwise noted.

Future developments. For the latest information about developments related to Form W-9 and its instructions, such as legislation enacted after they were published, go to *www.irs.gov/FormW9.*

Purpose of Form

An individual or entity (Form W-9 requester) who is required to file an information return with the IRS must obtain your correct taxpayer identification number (TIN) which may be your social security number (SSN), individual taxpayer identification number (ITIN), adoption taxpayer identification number (ATIN), or employer identification number (EIN), to report on an information return the amount paid to you, or other amount reportable on an information return. Examples of information returns include, but are not limited to, the following.

• Form 1099-INT (interest earned or paid)

• Form 1099-DIV (dividends, including those from stocks or mutual funds)

• Form 1099-MISC (various types of income, prizes, awards, or gross proceeds)

• Form 1099-B (stock or mutual fund sales and certain other transactions by brokers)

• Form 1099-S (proceeds from real estate transactions)

• Form 1099-K (merchant card and third party network transactions)

• Form 1098 (home mortgage interest), 1098-E (student loan interest), 1098-T (tuition)

• Form 1099-C (canceled debt)

• Form 1099-A (acquisition or abandonment of secured property)

Use Form W-9 only if you are a U.S. person (including a resident alien), to provide your correct TIN.

If you do not return Form W-9 to the requester with a TIN, you might be subject to backup withholding. See What is backup withholding, later.

I ATTACHED THIS FORM BLANK TO MY LETTER OF ROGATORY AND A BLANK 1099 OID FORM WITH MY EIN NUMBER FROM IRS AND CERTIFICATE OF GOOD STANDING WITH THE STATE. IF YOU UNDERSTAND LIENS YOUR PARENT COMPANY LLC WILL PUT A LIEN AGAINST THE CHILDREN D/B/A BUSINESS

9696   ☐ VOID   ☐ CORRECTED

PAYER'S name, street address, city or town, state or province, country, ZIP or foreign postal code, and telephone no.		1 Original issue discount for this year $	OMB No. 1545-0117	Original Issue
			Form **1099-OID**	Discount
		2 Other periodic interest $	(Rev. October 2019)	
			For calendar year 20___	
PAYER'S TIN	RECIPIENT'S TIN	3 Early withdrawal penalty $	4 Federal income tax withheld $	Copy A
		5 Market discount $	6 Acquisition premium $	For
RECIPIENT'S name		7 Description		Internal Revenue Service Center
Street address (including apt. no.)				File with Form 1096.
City or town, state or province, country, and ZIP or foreign postal code		8 Original issue discount on U.S. Treasury obligations $	9 Investment expenses $	For Privacy Act and Paperwork Reduction Act Notice, see the current General Instructions for Certain Information Returns.
	FATCA filing requirement ☐	10 Bond premium $	11 Tax-exempt OID $	
Account number (see instructions)	2nd TIN not. ☐	12 State	13 State identification no.	14 State tax withheld $ $

Form **1099-OID** (Rev. 10-2019)   Cat. No. 14421R   www.irs.gov/Form1099OID   Department of the Treasury - Internal Revenue Service

Do Not Cut or Separate Forms on This Page — Do Not Cut or Separate Forms on This Page

---

SCHEDULE I (Form 990)	Grants and Other Assistance to Organizations, Governments, and Individuals in the United States	OMB No. 1545-0047
	Complete if the organization answered "Yes" on Form 990, Part IV, line 21 or 22.	**2020**
Department of the Treasury Internal Revenue Service	▶ Attach to Form 990. ▶ Go to www.irs.gov/Form990 for the latest information.	Open to Public Inspection

Name of the organization   Employer identification number

Part I General Information on Grants and Assistance

1 Does the organization maintain records to substantiate the amount of the grants or assistance, the grantees' eligibility for the grants or assistance, and the selection criteria used to award the grants or assistance?   ☐ Yes   ☐ No

2 Describe in Part IV the organization's procedures for monitoring the use of grant funds in the United States.

Part II Grants and Other Assistance to Domestic Organizations and Domestic Governments. Complete if the organization answered "Yes" on Form 990, Part IV, line 21, for any recipient that received more than $5,000. Part II can be duplicated if additional space is needed.

1 (a) Name and address of organization or government	(b) EIN	(c) IRC section (if applicable)	(d) Amount of cash grant	(e) Amount of non-cash assistance	(f) Method of valuation (book, FMV, appraisal)	(g) Description of noncash assistance	(h) Purpose of grant or assistance
(1)							
(2)							
(3)							
(4)							

Form **56**
(Rev. November 2017)
Department of the Treasury
Internal Revenue Service

Notice Concerning Fiduciary Relationship

▶ Go to *www.irs.gov/Form56* for instructions and the latest information.
(Internal Revenue Code sections 6036 and 6903)

OMB No. 1545-0013

Part I   Identification

Name of person for whom you are acting (as shown on the tax return)	Identifying number	Decedent's social security no.
JOHN DOE BRADY JR		

Address of person for whom you are acting (number, street, and room or suite no.)
YOUR ADDRESS HERE

City or town, state, and ZIP code (If a foreign address, see instructions.)
YOUR ADDRESS HERE

Fiduciary's name
JUDGES NAME (EXAMPLE: Jane Doe Judge D/B/A Marion County Court Judge)

Address of fiduciary (number, street, and room or suite no.)
COURT PHONE NUMBER

City or town, state, and ZIP code	Telephone number (optional)
COURTS TOWN STATE AND ZIP	(123) 2218929

Section A. Authority

1   Authority for fiduciary relationship. Check applicable box:
a ☐ Court appointment of testate estate (valid will exists)
b ☐ Court appointment of intestate estate (no valid will exists)
c ☐ Court appointment as guardian or conservator
d ☐ Valid trust instrument and amendments
e ☐ Bankruptcy or assignment for the benefit or creditors
f ☑ Other. Describe ▶ APPOINTMENT OF FIDUCIARY CREDITOR AND DEBTOR TO SETTLE ALL DEBTS
2a If box 1a or 1b is checked, enter the date of death ▶
b If box 1c—1f is checked, enter the date of appointment, taking office, or assignment or transfer of assets ▶

Section B. Nature of Liability and Tax Notices

3   Type of taxes (check all that apply): ☐ Income   ☐ Gift   ☑ Estate   ☐ Generation-skipping transfer   ☐ Employment
☐ Excise   ☑ Other (describe) ▶ SOCIAL SECURITY TRUST

4   Federal tax form number (check all that apply): a ☐ 706 series   b ☐ 709   c ☐ 940   d ☐ 941, 943, 944
e ☐ 1040, 1040-A, or 1040-EZ   f ☐ 1041   g ☐ 1120   h ☑ Other (list) ▶ 1099 OID AND FORM 990 FOR TANF GRANTS

5   If your authority as a fiduciary does not cover all years or tax periods, check here . . . . . ▶ ☑
and list the specific years or periods ▶ BIRTH YEAR OF CHILD UNTIL PRESENT DATE (EXAMPLE: 2010 - 2022)

For Paperwork Reduction Act and Privacy Act Notice, see separate instructions.   Cat. No. 16375I   Form **56** (Rev. 11-2017)

Part II   Revocation or Termination of Notice

Section A—Total Revocation or Termination

6   Check this box if you are revoking or terminating all prior notices concerning fiduciary relationships on file with the Internal
Revenue Service for the same tax matters and years or periods covered by this notice concerning fiduciary relationship   ▶ ☐
Reason for termination of fiduciary relationship. Check applicable box:
a ☐ Court order revoking fiduciary authority
b ☐ Certificate of dissolution or termination of a business entity
c ☑ Other. Describe ▶ APPOINTING HONOR BOUND DUTY BOUND FUDICIARY TO HELP OFFSET NATIONAL DEBT

Section B—Partial Revocation

7a Check this box if you are revoking earlier notices concerning fiduciary relationships on file with the Internal Revenue Service
for the same tax matters and years or periods covered by this notice concerning fiduciary relationship . . . . . . ▶ ☐
b Specify to whom granted, date, and address, including ZIP code.
▶

Section C—Substitute Fiduciary

8   Check this box if a new fiduciary or fiduciaries have been or will be substituted for the revoking or terminating fiduciary and
specify the name(s) and address(es), including ZIP code(s), of the new fiduciary(ies) . . . . ▶ ☐
▶

Part III   Court and Administrative Proceedings

Name of court (if other than a court proceeding, identify the type of proceeding and name of agency)			Date proceeding initiated	
NAME OF THE COURT				
Address of court			Docket number of proceeding	
COURT ADDRESS			COURT CASE NUMBER	
City or town, state, and ZIP code	Date	Time		Place of other proceedings
COURT TOWN, COURT STATE, COURT ZIP CODE	DATE	☐ a.m. ☐ p.m.		

Part IV   Signature

Please Sign Here	I certify that I have the authority to execute this notice concerning fiduciary relationship on behalf of the taxpayer.		
	▶ _____ Fiduciary's signature	MANAGING MEMBER _____ Title, if applicable	_____ Date

Form **56** (Rev. 11-2017)

Department of the Treasury
Internal Revenue Service

Dear [IRS agent name of wo/man], Date: _____

As the Principal and owner of Treasury Direct Account # _____ & Name.
I request you file the Federal tax forms 1041, 1066, 1099-A, 1099 O.I.D. and 1096 for
1989 - 2020 tax period(s)Year(s) in question and any other returns that are due for me.

Please file the liabilities as taxable income to me, but omit filing or posting deductions against
the taxable income to me or making adjustments to dilute the liability on taxable income as, that
is a conflict of interest. This request is for return for settlement and closing in exchange Treasury
Direct Account # _____

On the 1099 O.I.D. the correction box at the top should be checked and also the Treasury Direct
Number # _____ is to be placed as the account number at the bottom of the
1099
O.I.D. form under Recipient to prevent identity theft and the account being intercepted and
diverted (deferred) if left open.

By:_____

Authorized Representative

AFFIDAVIT OF INDIVIDUAL SURETY
(See instructions on reverse)

OMB No.: **9000-0001**

Public reporting burden for this collection of information is estimated to average 3 hours per response, including the time for reviewing instructions, searching existing data sources; gathering and maintaining the data needed, and completing and reviewing the collection of information. Send comments regarding this burden estimate or any other aspect of this collection of information, including suggestions for reducing this burden, to the Regulatory Secretariat (MVA), Office of Acquisition Policy, GSA, Washington, DC 20405.

STATE OF G E O R G I A

COUNTY OF FULTON

SS.

I, the undersigned, being duly sworn, depose and say that I am: (1) the surety to the attached bond(s); (2) a citizen of the United States; and of full age and legally competent. I also depose and say that, concerning any stocks or bonds included in the assets listed below, that there are no restrictions on the resale of these securities pursuant to the registration provisions of Section 5 of the Securities Act of 1933. I recognize that statements contained herein concern a matter within the jurisdiction of an agency of the United States and the making of a false, fictitious or fraudulent statement may render the maker subject to prosecution under Title 18, United States Code Sections 1001 and 494. This affidavit is made to induce the United States of America to accept me as surety on the attached bond.

1. NAME *(First, Middle, Last) (Type or Print)* JEFFERY WAYNE MCBRIDE JR	2. HOME ADDRESS *(Number, Street, City, State, ZIP Code)* 1101 E CUMBERLAND AVE STE 201H-108 TAMPA, FL 33602
3. TYPE AND DURATION OF OCCUPATION	4. NAME AND ADDRESS OF EMPLOYER *(If Self-employed, so State)* FULTON COUNTY SUPERIOR COURT 136 PRYOR ST ATLANTA, GEORGIA 30303
5. NAME AND ADDRESS OF INDIVIDUAL SURETY BROKER USED *(If any)* *(Number, Street, City, State, ZIP Code)*	6. TELEPHONE NUMBER HOME – 480-573-4879 BUSINESS -480-573-4879

7. THE FOLLOWING IS A TRUE REPRESENTATION OF THE ASSETS I HAVE PLEDGED TO THE UNITED STATES IN SUPPORT OF THE ATTACHED BOND:

(a) Real estate *(Include a legal description, street address and other identifying description; the market value; attach supporting certified documents Including recorded lien; evidence of title and the current tax assessment of the property. For market value approach, also provide a current appraisal.)* SEE CASE #2105257

(b) FULTON COUNTY SUPERIOR COURT 136 PRYOR ST ATLANTA, GA 30303

(c) Assets other than real estate *(describe the assets, the details of the escrow account, and attach certified evidence thereof).*

CERTIFICATE OF IDENTITY DEPT. OF TREASURY FOR BUREAU OF THE PUBLIC DEBT PEACE BOND

8. IDENTIFY ALL MORTGAGES, LIENS, JUDGEMENTS, OR ANY OTHER ENCUMBRANCES INVOLVING SUBJECT ASSETS INCLUDING REAL ESTATE TAXES DUE AND PAYABLE.

SEE CASE **#21CP200858** CITATION # C-74468 & C-74469 FULTON COUNTY SUPERIOR COURT 136 PRYOR ST ATLANTA, GA 30303

9. IDENTIFY ALL BONDS, INCLUDING BID GUARANTEES, FOR WHICH THE SUBJECT ASSETS HAVE BEEN PLEDGED WITHIN 3 YEARS PRIOR TO THE DATE OF EXECUTION OF THIS AFFIDAVIT.

SEE CRIMINAL CASE **#21CP200858** CITATION # C-74468 & C-74469 FULTON COUNTY SUPERIOR COURT 136 PRYOR ST ATLANTA, GA 30303

DOCUMENTATION OF THE PLEDGED ASSET MUST BE ATTACHED.

10. SIGNATURE	11. BOND AND CONTRACT TO WHICH THIS AFFIDAVIT RELATES SEE OPTIONAL FORMS 90 AND 91 AND STANDARD FORMS 24, 25 AND 25A

12. SUBSCRIBED AND SWORN TO BEFORE ME AS FOLLOWS:		
a. DATE OATH ADMINISTERED MONTH　　DAY　　YEAR	b. CITY AND STATE *(Or other jurisdiction)*	Official Seal
c. NAME AND TITLE OF OFFICIAL ADMINISTERING OATH *(Type or print)*	d. SIGNATURE *(signature of notary public)*	e. MY COMMISSION EXPIRES

AUTHORIZED FOR LOCAL REPRODUCTION Previous edition is not usable

STANDARD FORM 28 (REV. 6/2003) Prescribed by GSA-FAR (48 CFR) 53.228(e)

An **Unrebutted Affidavit** Becomes the Judgment in Commerce **an Affidavit must be answered unlike a motion. EVERY STATE HAS A SMILIAR FORM BE SURE TO FIND ONE OR SIMPLY JUST CREATE YOUR OWN SIMILAR IN NATURE WITH THE SAME HEADING AND TITLE AFFIDAVIT FOR TERMINATION OF CHILD SUPPORT**

IN THE _____ JUDICIAL CIRCUIT, _____ COUNTY, MISSOURI

Judge or Division:	Case Number:
	MACSS Case ID:
Petitioner:	Petitioner's Address:
SSN (last four digits) or DOB: vs.	
Respondent:	Respondent's Address:
SSN (last four digits) or DOB:	(Date File Stamp)

Affidavit for Termination of Child Support
(This form may be used <u>only</u> where a claim is made that <u>no</u> child remains entitled to support.)

I, _____, am ☐ receiving support ☐ paying support for _____
(hereinafter referred to as the child), whose age is _____ and who is no longer entitled to support because:

(Check **all** which are applicable):

☐ The child died on _____ (date).

☐ The child married on _____ (date).

☐ The child entered active duty in the military on _____ (date).

☐ The child has become self-supporting, and the custodial parent has relinquished the child from parental control by express or implied consent.

☐ The child has attained the age of 21.

☐ The child is enrolled in and attending a secondary (high) school program of instruction but has attained the age of 21.

☐ The child has attained the age of 18 and

    ☐ has not graduated from secondary (high) school or completed a graduation equivalence degree program and, upon reaching age 18, was not attending and progressing toward completion of a secondary (high) school program of instruction.

    ☐ has graduated from secondary (high) school or completed a graduation equivalence degree program but did not enroll in an institution of vocational or higher education by October 1 following graduation or completion of the graduation equivalence degree program.

    ☐ has enrolled in an institution of vocational or higher education by October 1 following graduation from secondary (high) school or completion of a graduation equivalence degree program, but failed to achieve grades sufficient to re-enroll at such institution or failed to complete sufficient credit hours in each semester (at least 12 semester hours or the equivalent).

    ☐ when enrolled and attending an institution of vocational or higher education (course load of at least 12 hours), received failing grades in half or more of his/her course load in any one semester.

    ☐ when enrolled and attending an institution of vocational or higher education, the child failed to provide the non-custodial parent with documentation of grades from the education institution as requested by the non-custodial parent.

☐ The child is not physically or mentally incapacitated from supporting himself or herself, and the child's circumstances do not manifestly dictate that child support should continue.

☐ Other: _____.

I swear/affirm under the penalty of perjury that these facts are true to my best knowledge and belief.

_____   _____
Signature of Person Paying/Receiving Support   Date

Notice to Parent Receiving Support

If you agree with the statements in this Affidavit and agree to termination of the obligation to pay support for the child, you may, but are not required to, file an Acknowledgement with the court. Upon your filing of an Acknowledgement, a judgment terminating the obligation to pay support for the child will be entered.

If you disagree with the statements in this Affidavit and object to termination of the obligation to pay support for the child, you must file with the court an Answer which states the reasons the obligation to pay support for the child should continue. Upon your filing of an Answer, the court will treat this Affidavit as a request for hearing.

Your failure to file an Acknowledgment or Answer with the court within 30 days of your receipt of this Affidavit may result in entry by default of a judgment terminating the obligation to pay support for the child.

Certificate of Service of Parent Receiving Support

I certify that on _____ (date), I filed the original Affidavit with the circuit clerk of

_____ (County/City of St. Louis), Missouri, at _____ (address),

and mailed a copy to _____ (name), the parent paying support,

at _____ (address), _____ (city), _____ (state).

_____
Signature of Parent Receiving Support

Sheriff's or Server's Return

I certify that I served this Affidavit at _____ (address) in

_____ (County/City of St. Louis), Missouri, on _____ (date), at _____ (time), by:

(Check one)

☐ delivering a copy of the Affidavit and Answer and Acknowledgement forms to _____ (name);

☐ leaving a copy of the Affidavit and Answer and Acknowledgement forms at the dwelling place or usual abode of

_____ (name), with _____ (name), a

person of _____ (name)'s family over the age of 15 years who

permanently resides with the individual to be served.

☐ other: (describe) _____.

_____   _____
Printed Name of Sheriff or Server   Sheriff or Server

Must be sworn before a notary public if not served by an authorized officer.

(Seal)   Subscribed and sworn to before me on _____ (date).

My commission expires: _____   _____
                                                    Date   Notary Public

Sheriff's Fee (if applicable)
Service Fee $_____
Sheriff's Deputy Salary
Supplemental Surcharge $____10.00_____
Mileage $_____ (_____ miles @ $._____ per mile)
Total $_____

_____
Sheriff or Server

1) I am authorized to serve process in civil actions within the state or territory where the Affidavit was served.

2) My official title is _____ of _____ County, _____ (state).

3) I have served the above Affidavit by: (check one)

☐ delivering a copy of the Affidavit and Answer and Acknowledgement forms to _____ (name);

☐ leaving a copy of the Affidavit and Answer and Acknowledge forms at the dwelling place or usual abode of

_____ (name), with _____ (name),

a person of _____ (name)'s family over the age of 15 years who

permanently resides with the individual to be served.

☐ other: (describe) _____.

Served at _____ (address) in

_____ County, _____ (state), on _____ (date) at _____ (time).

_____   _____
Printed Name of Sheriff or Server   Sheriff or Server

Subscribed and sworn before me this _____ (date).

I am: (check one)   ☐ the clerk of the court of which affiant is an officer.
                              ☐ the judge of the court of which affiant is an officer.
                              ☐ authorized to administer oaths in the state in which the affiant served the above Affidavit. (use
                                 for out-of-state officer)
                              ☐ authorized to administer oaths. (use for court-appointed server)

(Seal)

_____
Signature and Title

Directions to Officer Making Return on Service of Affidavit

A copy of the Affidavit must be served on each person. If any person refuses to receive the copy of the Affidavit when offered to him, the return shall be prepared to show the offer of the officer to deliver the Affidavit and the person's refusal to receive the same.

Service shall be made: (1) On Individual. On an individual, including an infant or incompetent person not having a legally appointed guardian, by delivering a copy of the Affidavit to the individual personally or by leaving a copy of the Affidavit at the individual's dwelling house or usual place of abode with some person of the family over 15 years of age who permanently resides with the individual to be served, or by delivering a copy of the Affidavit to an agent authorized by appointment or required by law to receive service of process; (2) On Guardian. On an infant or incompetent person who has a legally appointed guardian, by delivering a copy of the Affidavit to the guardian personally.

Service may be made by an officer or deputy authorized by law to serve process in civil actions within the state or territory where such service is made.

Service may be made in any state or territory in the United States. If served in a territory, substitute the word "territory" for the word "state."

If service is made outside of Missouri, the officer making the service must swear an affidavit before the clerk, deputy clerk, or judge of the court of which the person is an officer or other person authorized to administer oaths. This affidavit must state the time, place, and manner of service, the official character of the affiant, and the affiant's authority to serve process in civil actions within the state or territory where service is made.

The return should be made promptly.

DUE PROCESS AS TAUGHT BY DON KILAM
What I did to get off child support and enforce due process

GET ALL DOCUMENTS NOTARAZIED

AFTER NOTARIZED

PUT TWO CENT STAMPS OR ANY STAMP WITH A NUMERIC VALUE NOT A FOREVER STAMP AND PLACE IT ON TOP RIGHT OF DOCUMENTS

AUTOGRAPH THRU THE STAMPS

AUTOGRAPH THE BACK OF THE DOCUMENT LIKE A CHECK

AUTOGRAPH AND DATE ALL RIGHTS RESERVED WITHOUT PREJUDICE

Attach form 56 fill out like illustration

Attach w9 and 1099 oid and grant form 990 THEY ARE TO BE LEFT BLANK

YOU CAN FILL IN THE sf 28 forms OR LEAVE blank

Attach promissory note as well and AUTOGRAPH and date back like a check

You no longer have to goto court return all mail to sender after blacking out YOUR NAME AS IT IS YOUR

NAME AND CAN NOT BE USED WITHOUT YOUR PERMISSION

SEND CERTIFIED MAIL TO THE CLERK OF CLERKS

MAKE SURE TO SENT TO HER NAME

EXAMPLE

Jane Doe d/b/a Illinois County Clerk

Then I would send a copy to the Federal District Courts Since they buy up the bonds and child support is a federal grant.

The State's Attorney as only Attorneys can give back rights during a war which this is a war as they are versus your estate.

Then I would start my 1099 OID process found in another book and send the case to the IRS the real court which is a tax court!

Then I would send copies to the Security Exchange Commission, The Federal and Trade Commission

And then The General Service Administration,

This is not legal advice if you need legal advice, please seek counsel this is for educational and informational and entertainment purposes only

Your Missouri Courts

Judicial Links | eFiling | Help | Contact Us | Print

Search for Cases by [Select Search Method ▾]

Logon

09MR-CV00391-02 - MO. F.S.D. V JEFFREY W MCBRIDE & ▓▓▓▓▓▓▓▓▓▓▓

| Case Header | Parties & Attorneys | Docket Entries | Charges, Judgments & Sentences | Service Information | Filings Due | Scheduled Hearings & Trials | Civil Judgments | Garnishments/ Execution |

Sort Date Entries: ⦿ Descending ○ Ascending   Display Options: [All Entries ▾]

04/30/2015	**Correspondence Sent**
	copy of Judgment mailed to both parties at last known addresses copy mailed to FSPC-copy given to Atty Rapp
	Judgment Entered
	#26 Judgment Terminating Child Support on Ava entered as per memo JUDGE JOHN J JACKSON
04/29/2015	**Affidavit of Termination CS**
	#25 Acknowledgment Agreeing to Termination of Child Support on ▓▓ 08/21/07 s▓▓▓▓▓▓▓▓▓CP filed
	Filed By: ▓▓▓▓▓IRENE ELLER
04/16/2015	**Return Service on Affidavit**
	#24 Affidavit for Termination of Child Support returned by Marion County Sheriff showing service to Respondent on 4/15/15 filed. Document ID - 15-SAFI-1, Served To - ▓▓▓▓▓▓▓▓▓ IRENE; Server - SO MARION COUNTY-PALMYRA; Served Date - 15-APR-15; Served Time - 15:08:00; Service Type - Sheriff Department, Reason Description - Served
04/14/2015	**Affidavit Issued**
	Document ID: 15-SAFI-1, for ▓▓▓▓▓▓▓▓▓▓▓
03/25/2015	**Affidavit of Termination CS**
	#23
	Filed By: JEFFREY W MCBRIDE

AFFIDAVIT DATE
STARTS AT DOB OF CHILD

IF YOU NEED ONE ON ONE COACHING

TEXT 480-573-4879

OR EMAIL support@malikkilam.com

Made in the USA
Columbia, SC
14 November 2024

46506442R00046